3rd Compass
Navigating Reality and the Last Days

Ty Alexander Huynh

MainstreamMedia

3rd Compass

Published in Rosemount, MN by Mainstream Media
Distributed by Bethany Press International

First printing, November 2009

ISBN: 978-0-578-04003-5

Unless otherwise indicated, Scripture quotations are taken from the *Holy Bible: New International Version*, copyright © 1973, 1978, 1984 by International Bible Society.

Cover design: Ty Alexander Huynh

Printed in the United States of America

Dedicated to Truth, Wisdom, and Knowledge.
May you find them within...

Contents

Foreword

What is reality, really? All of us have our own perspectives about the universe we live in. Our personal experiences and knowledge make our view of reality very subjective, but isn't there only one true reality? That is the absolute reality the *3rd Compass* aims to highlight. It is the reality we all share together, and no matter how you may view it, our places in it remain the same.

This reality is so vast and has so many layers that measuring and understanding it completely is nearly impossible. The *3rd Compass* does not try to explain everything about our reality – all the physics, the chemistry, the biology, and philosophy. The sciences cannot be wholly conveyed in one book.

However, the sheer amount of information is not why this book focuses more on one topic or another. The *3rd Compass* was written to bring a more complete understanding to the most important aspects of our true reality – the ones that explain all the rest and that have the most impact on us and our lives.

This book dismantles the modern age's tendency to prefer scientific facts and methods over everything else. This does not mean logic and reason are thrown out the window. On the contrary, the *3rd Compass* explains exactly why the scientific view of reality is insufficient and actually incapable of understanding our absolute reality. In fact, science and logic are used extensively in this book to support that true picture of reality – the Big Picture.

It is only in the Big Picture of Reality that meaning to our existence can be seen. But not only that, it gives us the reasons for so many things that science cannot explain, such as why there is suffering

and hardship in our world, why we struggle within and between
ourselves, and even the reasons for the universal laws of morality.

The Big Picture resolves the debate between science and God,
Darwinian Evolution and Creationism, one religion over another,
and other topics of conflict in the debates of life, nature, reality,
and religion. The *3rd Compass* aims to encompass everything into
one single framework so that we can see the reasons behind it all
– something science cannot do. So, if you are interested at all in these
debates and the meaning of your life and everything else, then read on.

Ty Alexander Huynh

1st Compass

Direction

*A*nyone who needs to know where they are going must have a good sense of direction. What kind of people would we be without it? Adventurers who always get lost, navigators who lead their captains to the wrong ports, and yes, drivers who always tell their passengers, "I'm not lost. I just like taking 'short cuts!'" Some of us have a better sense of direction than others, but it is certain that anyone who is blindfolded and placed in the middle of an unknown landscape will need help to get their bearings and proceed in the right direction.

Getting those bearings is why we have our first group of compasses – instruments that tell us what direction to go, such as a Boy Scout's trusty pocket compass, which points in geographic north, or a seaman's sextant, which measures latitude and longitude by using the stars. These instruments give us a better sense of our bearings, clues to our location relative to the environment, so that we have a good sense of which direction to proceed.

These compasses help us find our way when we are lost or uncertain of our location. In the same way, there are compasses which help us proceed in the right direction through a different kind of landscape – that of our lives. I will call this landscape your life map because it contains not just your location in the world but your decisions and circumstances. Because of this, your map is boundless in area but bounded in time. This means that your life has infinite possibilities but the paths in it always move forward in time so that you cannot move backwards along the path you have taken.

Oh, how so many of us have wished we could go backward in time – a few minutes, hours or even years to correct a bad decision. Some of us have been plagued by bad decisions and missteps on our life map, but among all the possible circumstances and outcomes on our map, there is also an ideal path – the one that leads to our ultimate happiness, sense of right, or contentment. Some people call this their destiny, but whether you believe in destiny is not important here. What **is** important is that there is **always** a way to move onto that ideal path.

How can we do this on a life map, though? Navigating most maps is a straight forward task. You simply follow the roads, landmarks, and signs that lead you to your destination. Our life maps also have roads, landmarks, and signs to guide us. The routes through our life map, though, have roads we pave ourselves through the decisions we make.

The landmarks are there as well – the significant events in our lives like the first time we fell in love, our high school graduation, or getting our first "real" job after college. These landmarks can be used for navigation, but they are generally not specific enough to make further decisions by. What we need are signs, which are more specific in pointing us in the right direction.

Wouldn't it be grand if we had signs, like road signs, that materialized in the real world and told us the right steps to take and decisions to make? Ask that person out to lunch, study this in school, take that job, or move to this place.

Unfortunately, those literal signs don't exist in the real world. What we have is more subtle and the origins can be mysterious, but the goal of this book is to unveil the cloud that shrouds these mysteries, and ultimately, to help you see those signs and navigate your life map with clarity.

One step at a time, though. We are speaking of signs at this moment and another definition of signs besides the literal board on a post is that of things which represent something else. It can be any thing or grouping of things that hint to a greater meaning – clues to something more, for example the symbol consisting of an exclamation point inside a triangle is a sign for a warning or hazard. Signs are more varied than symbols, though. They can also be unlikely coincidences or series of coincidences, events, feelings or "nudgings" that seem to be linked for a purpose. This purpose may be to help you in some way or to act as a guide. These are the road signs we want for navigating our life map.

This sounds mysterious, like divining your future from sticks thrown in the air, but what I speak of is not some silly arbitrary ritual nor is it about getting meaning out of meaningless things – connecting dots that should not be connected, like choosing to go to Collins Crew College because it rhymes with blue, your favorite color.

What I speak of is listening. Listening harder and paying closer attention to the things around you, and then taking notice of what stands out and "speaks" to you. I know, this still sounds mysterious. You may ask, just what are we listening to? But the right question is, **who** are we listening to?

This is where you more science-minded readers may start to balk, but bear with me. This book is aimed at unveiling the clouds that obscure supposedly "irrational" things with solid reasoning and understandable logic. Things are only irrational if you do not understand their causes, but once you understand, the fog is lifted and objects of obscurity can come into focus.

Passing Signs

To help illustrate an example of "listening," here is a story based on true events and real people, though names have been changed. John and Linda were engaged to be married. They were in a photographer's studio to look over his work and see if he was a good fit for the wedding photos.

After an hour of looking at scores of photos full of perfectly groomed and dressed people, flowers, dimple-cheeked children, frumpy puppies, and poofed-up cats with bows in their fur (many of which seemed to be scowling, by the way), the couple began to leave the studio in good spirits and with hope for their future.

As John and Linda walked arm in arm towards their car, they noticed a few people standing next to it – an older gentleman, a young man and a teenager. The young man noticed the couple and approached them and asked, "Do you own this car here?" He pointed to Linda's white sedan.

John and Linda acknowledged, "Yes," and the young man said, "I don't know how to break this to you, but these fellows," he looked towards the gentleman and teenager, "hit your car. I was walking along and saw it. Your car doesn't look drivable."

The witness gestured the couple to walk to the other side of the car facing the street where they saw the front side smashed in and the top of the front wheel bent inwards. John thought, "Yeah, obviously not drivable."

The witness continued, "We waited for you to come back for a while and those guys wanted to leave, but I made them stay. The kid was driving the car and he was making a right turn onto the street here, trying to get ahead of oncoming cars so he put on the gas, but then he just seemed to loose control and smashed into your car."

John and Linda thanked the witness for staying and offering his help. They took down everyone's information and called for a tow truck and family member to pick them up. While they waited, John's mind wandered and he thought it was extraordinarily bad luck this would happen, but accidents happen. Move on.

The following week, John and Linda were shopping for the wedding again and had bought a pair of crystal champagne flutes. They took them to an engraver and had their names and the date of the wedding engraved on the glasses. They were rimmed with gold, had elongated vertical, diamond shaped indents all around the sides that made them sparkle, and the flowing engraved text made them all the more beautiful to behold.

The flutes were wrapped up in bundles of tissue and paper and packaged securely in a box. When the couple got home, Linda wanted to show her mother how gorgeous the flutes were, so she took them out of the box and unwrapped them, but they saw that one of the flutes was broken. A whole side of it had cracked and broke away. Linda gasped, "Oh no! How could this happen? They were packaged so nicely."

John said, "That's awful!" and thought that's not good but glasses break. No big deal. "We'll get it replaced. It won't be a problem," he reassured her.

The broken flute was replaced, but the strange thing was that many more things about the wedding went awry. It is certainly a stressful and overwhelming time for many couples, but things that shouldn't go wrong, did. The caterer backed out at the last minute, dresses were torn inexplicably, and John was nearly an hour late to the ceremony because his ride was lost. It seemed that something was against John and Linda. Even though the wedding was not a smooth operation, the couple did get married and began a life together.

What John and Linda did not know was that their marriage was to fail three years later because they had constant arguments and disagreements about how to live life, spend money, and raise their child.

The real problem with the marriage was that the couple had passed the signs of trouble before the wedding and ignored them. They overlooked not just the unlucky, coincidental things, like the auto accident, broken glass and wedding problems, but also the problems in their relationship.

What they failed to realize was that the coincidental problems were actually signs to look closer at their decision to marry. John's thoughts that the auto accident and broken glass, both linked to getting married, were unlucky was not entirely off the mark. They were deliberate signs given to help guide them – to help them navigate their life maps – because the truth was that John and Linda had frequent arguments and disagreements before they were married.

The couple overlooked those things just like the coincidental signs because they thought all they really needed to be happy was love. They did have love in the beginning, but incompatibility and hostility erodes love, and for John and Linda their love for one another eroded until there was nothing left of their marriage to save.

The question remains, though. Who sent those coincidental signs? It wasn't some entity called Bad Luck or Destiny. The next story, also based on true events, will illuminate the Who better. It is a story about Bill Wilson or "Skip" who we will meet in greater detail with his amazing testimonials in Chapter Four.

Rigged to Live

Skip was working as a derrick hand on an oil drilling rig in the Gulf of Mexico. It was one of the first jack-up drilling rigs in use, which were like barges with three legs that could be lifted or lowered in and out of the water. The barge portion of the rig was the drilling platform where the majority of the drilling work was done.

The legs were lowered into the water and sunk into the sea floor to anchor the rig, as well as raise or "jack-up" the drilling platform above the surface of the water so operations would not be disturbed by waves. When the rig needed to be moved, the legs were raised and the whole rig floated freely and was towed like a barge to a different location.

Skip's drilling rig was going to be moved in this way, and as a derrick hand, his duty was to be up on the central derrick or steel tower mast and remove sections of pipe from the drill as it was extracted from the ground.

Skip stepped on the ladder to take his station as he had done many times before, but today, about 10 feet up the ladder, he felt something touch his shoulders and rest on them until he ascended the full 100 feet. When he got off the ladder, the slight weight on his shoulders left.

"Strange," he wondered, but then thought nothing more of it.

The next day he climbed the derrick again to work his shift and once more at about 10 feet up the ladder a weight rested on his shoulders except it was heavier than the day before and like yesterday it stayed until he got to the top, and then it was gone.

The third day Skip started up the ladder and again the weight came upon his shoulders, but it was so heavy this time that he struggled to get to the top. "What's going on?" he thought, "Am I getting tired that fast? Can't be. I'm used to climbing this thing with no problems."

He pondered this throughout his day but could not understand it. Wind does not feel like that, and at all other times he felt physically fine and not fatigued or weighted down. It was only when climbing up the ladder that this unusual feeling came.

On the fourth day, Skip hesitated for a moment and looked up the ladder wondering what would happen today. He grabbed the rungs and started his way up. This time though, at ten feet he was stopped completely. He tried to push his body up, but it seemed to be blocked by an invisible force holding his shoulders down.

Confused, he waved an arm about to feel the air around him. There was nothing, yet he could not ascend any further up the ladder with all the strength he could muster.

"How can this be?" Skip thought and went back down the ladder. He stood there for a few minutes and pondered, "Four days in a row a weight is put on my shoulders and it gets heavier each time and now today I can't go up at all." Well, Skip was a stubborn young man, but certainly not stupid.

He thought, "Somebody is trying to tell me something." So he went to his supervisor, the driller, and said, "I'm not feeling well. Can someone else work derricks today?"

The driller replied, "Sure, Wilson, just grab that drill sub and put it on the rack." Skip acknowledged and got the drill sub. The floor was covered in oily mud and slick from drilling operations. Skip was used to working in these conditions, though, and was cautious, but he walked a few steps with the drill sub and his footing gave way.

Before he knew it, he slid down 30 feet and out a pipe door. He tried to get up, but a pain shot through his back so they called for an emergency airlift to take him to the hospital.

The next morning as he was recovering in the hospital bed, Skip saw on the television screen a news flash scrolling across the bottom, "An oil drilling rig has sunk in the gulf killing the crew. We are not releasing names pending notification of family." Skip's rig, the Ocean Express, had sunk and he was the only crewman not onboard – the only survivor.

Who?

The two stories above illustrate that there are roads signs to help us navigate our life maps, but they are not just static symbols or arrows that point in a direction. They can interact with us, as well as simply guide or nudge us, to take into account more information than we normally would consider. But the question remains, Who are *They*?

Do you believe in guardian angels? What about angels, period? You may scoff at the idea of intelligent, invisible agents helping us through life but recent scientific surveys of the American public have found that 55 to 68 percent believe in angels.

To be more precise, a Baylor University study of 1,500 people found that 55 percent of people polled believe in guardian angels, and a separate study done by the Pew Forum of 35,000 people found that 68 percent believe that angels and demons (the angelic opposites) are active in the world.

These studies included people from all types of social class, education, ethnicity and religious belief, so the skewing in favor of a particular group cannot be a factor. Still, the majority believes in angels, yet a minority ever speak of their beliefs. Why is that?

It is not hard to understand why few people mention angels. In our modern age of scientific reason it seems counter intuitive to believe in the supernatural. It is akin to believing that fairies exist at the bottom of a garden or that werewolves roam the streets during a full moon. Preposterous! Yet the majority believes in angels.

Perhaps it is because there is evidence. There **are** signs and there **are** interactions – by people like Skip and you and me – everyday people.

"Why haven't I noticed anything then?" you may cry. Well, that is a question we will also try to answer later in this book. The next chapter involves the evidence and where it leads.

2nd Compass

Drafting Up

*N*o architect would be without a compass, nor artist, nor engineer. This second class of compasses help us draw up a circumference or measure a distance. Generally, these instruments are constructed of two, equal length rods connected at one end to pivot like scissors, so that circumferences or distances of different sizes can be measured or drawn.

I remember my first experience with a drawing compass in grade school art. We used it to fill pages of construction paper with circles of all sizes and colors, but my first page was filled with squiggly blobs that only resembled circles. I thought, "I should have drawn them freehand. It's useless!"

My hands have steadied since then and a draftsman's compass was often within arm's reach during my younger years as an architectural draftsman. It was a tool that I relied on often to gauge distances as well as draw perfect circles. It was used as much for measuring as it was for layout. In the same way, we can measure and lay out the things that seem like an unexplainable mess – things like the supernatural and angels – into a picture, or blueprint if you will, that is understandable and easy to read.

This is where science comes into play. What can science tell us about the meaning of life when it is such a subjective experience? No matter what your perception of reality is, there is only one absolute or true reality that is the same for everyone. Our personal realities are subjective, but once you step outside your own self and remove your tinted shades of perception the true reality in which we exist can be seen.

To paint this picture, I will use the tools and logic processes of scientific reasoning. Bear in mind that I say, "the tools and logic of scientific reasoning" as opposed to what the many fields of science or the scientific method (testing and proving through experimentation) have told us about reality.

The distinction is important because science over the centuries has painted a picture of the universe that obscures true reality, but the logic behind scientific reasoning can still be used to create a truer blueprint. Still, science is not all bad. It has produced many useful things and makes our lives easier. We have a more precise idea of how the mechanics of the universe work – how mass and energy are related or how biology and chemistry interact – but that portion of the whole is only what we have been able to probe and comprehend.

Consider that our view of the world and universe have changed drastically over the millennia. Even within the last one hundred years our concepts of physical reality have been profoundly changed by the works of theoretical physicists and other researchers.

We have gone from viewing our earth as the center of the universe or being carried on the back of a great tortoise to just being a speck of dust traveling through the cosmos at some 66,000 miles an hour. Why have our views changed so much?

It is because we conceptualize the universe only through what we can test or probe with our tools – be that our eyes and other senses of perception or devised tools, such as microscopes, telescopes, radio receivers and computers. That is how the scientific method works. We test and probe and revise and test and probe and revise until we are satisfied with the accuracy and consistency of the results.

But also consider that our tools can be inaccurate or unable to discern with the detail needed to see reality in its entirety. It is like the blind man only being able to conceptualize his world with a walking stick. How can he know what colors are like – the calm and majesty of blue or the intensity and passion of red? How can he know the beauty of a sunset on the ocean or the whimsy of a butterfly on the wind?

Likewise, our probes and experiments can only tell us a limited set of information, mainly that which they were designed for or are capable of telling us. Also consider that some things cannot be probed at all, either because we do not have the means or the understanding. Just like the blind from birth, how could we know light, color and images without vision?

Everything Is Meaningless

Science has blindfolded and misled us. That is not to say what we have learned from it is untrue or useless. What I mean is, it obscures our true reality such that we become unaware of or even deny the parts of reality that science cannot explain, and as a result we also deny the greater meaning of our own existence.

It is just as the blind man perceiving reality with only his walking stick – essential parts of reality are overlooked. Another term for this kind of perception is tunnel vision or what I like to call, **Selective Reasoning**. It exists because humans as limited beings who are exposed to a limited set of experiences and knowledge naturally prefer to see reality based on what we know.

We filter the world or **select** certain conclusions based on our personal knowledge base. Our tendency to do this is not only a product of our limited set of personal experiences and knowledge but also arises in part because of how our minds organize and process information.

Our brains work to bundle the millions of pieces of information we receive into a more simplified and organized structure so that it is more manageable. We basically categorize and link information to build a library inside our minds.

This helps us recall information quickly as well as link related concepts together like dogs and cats are mammals or doors are for passage into a different area and the handle on a door opens the door, therefore using the handle will give you access to the area behind the door. Our structured minds help us analyze the world quickly, but this has its problems as well. It leads to stereotypes and prejudgments – making conclusions based not on facts but on personal opinions.

This is Selective Reasoning and the problem with it in our discussion is that to understand true reality we need to be very broad in understanding, so the more we learn about one particular aspect of reality, like say, biology or psychology, the more skewed in that direction our perception becomes. Our tunnel vision goes into a tighter circle and our Selective Reasoning becomes even more selective.

When this happens, alternative solutions to problems are dismissed entirely because they do not make sense with what we are familiar with. That is the danger to seeing reality with the eyes of a specialist. By their very nature, specialists are more focused on a particular point of view. Through years of training and conditioning they are honed to excel in their field, but true reality is much wider than any single field of science or science in its entirety.

The reality that science gives us is nothing more than a giant collection of facts, formulas, and pieces of information – the Superlative Data Blob. It is impressive in size and scope and has many uses in its different data chunks, which correspond to the different branches of science, but ultimately as a whole, it is meaningless.

What we want is that blueprint of absolute reality – the truest picture of reality – which also lends meaning to everything in existence. Then by superimposing that blueprint onto our life maps we can also attain meaning and direction to our own lives. To draft that blueprint, though, we need more than science. We need to mold and change the Blob by adding solidifying agents and catalysts that will ultimately frame reality.

Laying Out the Next Ingredient

What are these agents and catalysts? One agent we need is another branch of science, Theology – the Science of God and Religion. Some naysayers who hear God or religion will start to balk and turn away at this point, but I would ask that they do not fall to logical hypocrisy and think that only rational things fall into the natural and physical sciences.

On the contrary, I aim to highlight the logic that makes God and religion essential to the framework. There are no smoke and mirrors or slight of hands involved here, and I hope that the rest of this chapter will lead those who seek true reality or Truth will start to bring it into focus.

A charge that many atheists have against theists is that believers are irrational to believe in invisible, intangible, and improvable entities such as angels or gods. Some atheists go so far as to call believers delusional. How do they come to these conclusions? It is simply Selective Reasoning.

They fail to realize that their own viewpoint is limited and tinted at the same time they accuse the other side of the same thing. They are overconfident in their own reasoning – that humans' tendency to believe in religion and gods is a product of evolution, gene propagation and/or social psychology, that unexplainable things can simply be dismissed as irrational or delusional, or that gods, angels and religion in general are fanciful ways of comprehending our existence.

This is understandable logic if all you include in your analysis are what the natural and physical sciences can tell, but that is far too selective a viewpoint and leads to conceit, because certainly, testing and proving can affirm theory and give confidence, but in true reality not all things can be tested and probed in this way. It is like the renowned physicist Albert Michelson proclaiming an end to physics at the end of the 19th century because the laws of the physical universe were thought to be known and well understood.

Even in this century, the drum beat of scientific confidence is back with superstring theory, which if proven correct, will unify currently separate divisions of physics into one architecture. Still, even if superstring theory is proven correct, isn't announcing the end of physics premature? Can nothing more be learned?

In the same vein, ardent atheists proclaim that believers hold to faith blindly – that they believe in fanciful things without evidence or taking all the information into account. But little do they know, they are guilty of the same. That is logical hypocrisy, and we are all capable of falling to it no matter what side we stand on.

Reality Proof – God or Science?

Scientists like to measure, test and prove. That is the scientific method and atheists likewise like to use this logic to disprove God and all things related. The logic goes, "Well, we can't measure gods or angels and we can't test for their existence, so we cannot prove their existence. Therefore, they do not exist and are products of human imagination."

Another strand of logic goes, "We tried to test for gods, angels and all kinds of supernatural things, like ESP, but our experiments did not prove anything inconclusively. Therefore, they do not exist and are products of human imagination."

Not so fast! Conclusions of this kind are products of Selective Reasoning. Remember earlier, I stated that we do not have the understanding or the means to probe certain aspects of reality. We are the blind trying to poke at reality with sticks to figure it out. This will always lead to an incomplete understanding and confound us. We need to rely on other evidence to get that blueprint of reality.

My first example of evidence deals with infinite random variance and the scientific theory that it is sufficient to account for our universe and life as we know it. It is a backbone for much belief in the reality that science paints as well as a pillar holding up another theory that atheists hold as proof against God and religion – Darwinian Evolution.

The theory goes something like this: Our universe is one out of infinite universes, all with different values for the laws of physics, which are simply set at random, and our universe is one out of presumably very few of the infinite variety that can produce what we see in the heavens as well as produce the kind of life forms that exist.

Physicists have studied the laws of physics for hundreds of years and now know that if certain parameters of the universe are changed just slightly, such as the strength of magnetic fields and nuclear forces, then our universe and life could not exist. It appears that our reality is just right to produce what we see in the universe as well as carbon based life, such as us, but a divine being or creator behind it all can be dismissed because of infinite random variance.

This is an application of the anthropic principle, which when applied to this context states that our universe is as it is and we exist simply because we happen to reside in a universe that has the right parameters set – a chance, lucky fluke – and not because our universe or life was designed with any particular goal in mind.

This is an interesting idea, but the fact is, it is only that – an idea, an unproven theory thought up to try and explain our existence. There is nothing else to back up this theory and no evidence of infinite universes. Superstring theorists who know the power of multiple dimensions certainly cannot make a claim for multiple universes, nor can proponents of quantum mechanics, a division of physics that tells us matter and energy can exist in multiple states at the same time.

There is simply no evidence of alternate universes, much less an infinite variety, in experiment or in formula. I charge that these ideas of infinite universes and the sufficiency of infinite random variance are not just unproven theories but also wishful thinking.

The Artist's Proof

Let us examine the concept of infinite random variance more closely so that it is easier to see why it is insufficient to create the reality we exist in – our universe, the laws of physics, and DNA based life. Advocates of infinite random variety always bring up examples like a chimpanzee (let's call him

A grayscale version of San Giorgio may be easier to produce using only infinite random variance.
(see Insert 1 for color reproduction)

Charlie) punching away at a typewriter ad infinitum will eventually produce the works of Shakespeare, or my favorite variant, Charlie with a paint brush and palette blotting away at a canvas forever will some day produce a work of Da Vinci like the Mona Lisa.

Well, let's make it easier on Charlie. He might have a better chance of producing a work in the impressionist style like "San Giorgio Maggiore at Dusk" by Monet (see figure above) since the brush strokes used in this style are more akin to the simple blotting and short uncalculated strokes that Charlie is capable of producing. Plus, San Giorgio seems to be a simple portrait compared to other works with much more complicated detail.

Let us make it even easier for Charlie by giving him only two colors to deal with, black and white, to try and produce a grayscale version of the painting. We will also blindfold Charlie and give him a robotic shoulder, arm, and hand with no handicaps since the rule of the game is that there can be no rules or predispositions to direct the portrait other than complete, uniform randomness and infinite time. A seeing and fully biological Charlie would have the tendency to group strokes together a certain way even though a supposedly "unthinking" Charlie has no projected agenda, he is still subject to interference and limitations created through his biomechanical nature.

Now we will get blind, bionic Charlie started. As we watch him applying stroke after stroke, some are simply dots while others are short lines or arcs. Some are thick while others are thin depending on the pressure applied to the brush, but after hundreds and thousands and millions and billions of strokes swiped we see that the picture we have

does not change much from the initial point when the canvas was saturated with strokes. It is a random grouping of light and dark blotches, which as a whole resembles a fuzzy blown up photo of an old style, 20th century television set showing white noise (see figure at right).

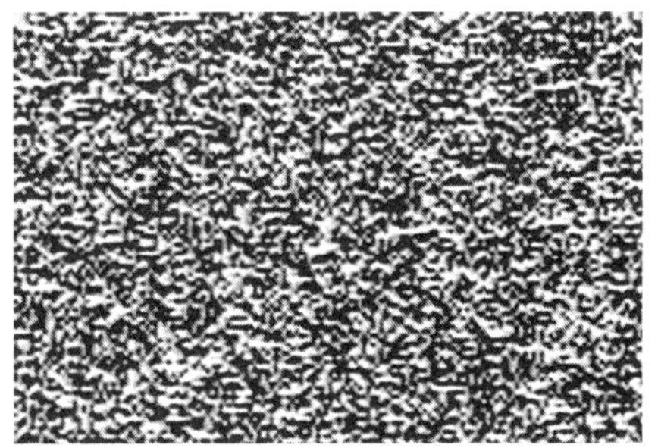

The product of uniform random variance – white noise.

There is nothing like Monet's skyline of San Giorgio. There are no groupings of darkness that resemble the sharp, blocked off sections for the steeple and cityscape, nor the rhythmic combinations of strokes to make the ripples of water, nor the gentle transition of darker to lighter strokes from the horizontal center to the bottom, which shows the gradations from dark horizon to light sky in the water's reflection.

The only resemblance that random variance gives to the original painting is in the black and white version of Venice's sunset sky, and even then it is only a minor resemblance. We can see that our rules of uniform randomness are not sufficient to paint a portrait even as "simple" as San Giorgio.

Now, if we give Charlie just a few colors to work with, such as the painter's primaries – blue, red, and yellow – in order that he may have a chance to make a color reproduction of the painting, we will see that he fails even more miserably, because without conscious and calculated application of color and pressure the canvas will simply turn out to be a random mess of gray-brown, red, blue, yellow, orange, violet, and green blotches (the result of mixing the primary colors together in full, in part, or not at all). This is simply a colorized version of the white noise canvas. Can you see what is wrong with the pure random approach?

The problem is randomness itself. It is incapable of producing what we want no matter how long a time span we give it. To illustrate this further, consider a more finite and simple canvas and artist. A computer program to reproduce a small version of Monet's painting on a virtual canvas, a grid, 300 pixels wide by 200 pixels high (a pixel is one colored block on the virtual canvas). Let's only use the colors needed to make the painting as well – various shades of blue, red, yellow and orange. The program will simply go through every pixel on the canvas in order and assign it a color at random, or if you want full randomness, the program can select a pixel at random instead of going through one by one. It does not matter, because the outcome of randomness anywhere in the formula will produce the same result.

Any good computer programmer will be able to predict the outcome of this program. All the images produced will be a colorized version of the white noise canvas just as we saw when Charlie painted with color. The problem once more is the whole notion of random. Its very nature is that it has no structure, organization, or direction, and to ask it to produce structure or organization, which is clearly needed in any work of art, is not only wishful thinking but simply impossible.

To make a work of art, an artist needs to apply color in a calculated and deliberate way. His or her technique must be structured to create the desired effect – rules need to be followed to meet the end. Certain colors must go in certain places in a certain order, amount, direction, etc. A good writer also needs this kind of structure. Words are composed of letters that must go in a certain order and sentences are composed of words that also must have an order and the entire story itself must have a structured order. It is structure upon structure upon structure and introducing random into any or all parts of the equation will destroy the desired outcome. No chimp Charlie could become a Shakespeare or a Monet, and on the same order, no amount of random universe jumbling can produce our universe, which is also built structure upon structure.

In the classical view of physics these structures are subatomic particles, which come together to form matter (atoms), energy, and force (magnetic and electric), which in turn come together with the other fundamental laws of physics such as gravity to form molecules, stars, planets and life. In a more modern view of physics with superstring theory, the first structures are minuscule, multidimensional vibrating strings that are set to vibrate in certain ways to create the subatomic particles as well as all the other known forces, such as gravity and electromagnetism – structure upon structure upon structure. How do you think so much structure can be had without intelligent design?

The only way to make infinite, random variance work in these cases is to take random completely out and replace it with an ordered assault. Charlie would have to systematically type every single possible combination of letters, numbers, symbols and spaces that could fill 100 pages of text (what is needed for one of Shakespeare's works), and one of those millions and billions of 100 page books will have a work of Shakespeare in it. Likewise, if the computer program were set to draw every single image possible using that small, finite canvas and color set, there will be a small set of images out of the billions that resemble Monet's work.

Now this is an idea that scientists could cling to in order to have our universe exist. They need a whole set of alternate universes with the laws of physics set at every other possible value, but isn't that idea just as wishful as the infinite random variance theory? Why would there even be a whole set of universes laid out in such a neat and systematic way without intelligent intervention? Let us not forget also that there is no evidence for alternate universes, an infinite number or otherwise.

Also consider that there are absolutely no instances of infinite or infinitesimal (the infinitely small) anywhere in our natural universe. Infinity is a mathematical and theoretical concept only. In the real world, there is an upper and lower bound to everything. Not even the speed of light is infinite, nor the size or age of the universe, nor the size of atoms or superstrings. Why then would there be an infinite number of universes?

To support such a notion you would be faced with concocting theories that are clearly not supported by any scientific evidence or reasonable logic. The most logical choice for an atheist would be to abandon the whole infinite or "every possible combination" universes theory if they want to hold true to their belief that only scientifically proven or even plausible things can be true.

Circling Smaller and Smaller

Now that infinite random variance has been shown to be incapable of creating structure, let us look at further evidence for an intelligent creator. Our reality is full of logical structure everywhere we look. The laws of physics are so structured that we have been able to replicate them with mathematical formulas. Structure – It is everywhere from the formation of the galaxies to the stems and veins of the leaves on the trees.

It can be argued that all these examples of structure are not a result of intelligent design but of the great possibilities given by the laws of physics and the workings of DNA-based life. You could try that tact, but it is not a sufficient argument. All of these structures are built upon smaller and smaller structures, just as a book is built on chapters, which are built on paragraphs, which are built on sentences, which are built on words, which are built on letters, and from the smallest component onward there is intelligent design to imbue each component with meaning.

Furthermore, one must combine these components with rules and laws, which involves further intelligent design. You cannot just willy-nilly mix components at random as I have explained in the last section. To successfully argue zero intelligent design, you must go down to the smallest structures in physics and life in order to see if these building blocks can possibly not have any intelligent design for them to work.

Consider DNA itself, the building blocks for all life as we know it. In its simplest definition it is a code consisting of the pairings of four chemical compounds, adenine to thymine and cytosine to guanine, which when strung together in a sequence defines an organism's characteristics – how it is built, grows and dies – essentially the code of life.

Most atheists would suggest that DNA is just another random fluke resulting from a lucky mixing of these chemicals in a liquid water bath, but also consider that DNA has structured properties far beyond the simple pairing of chemicals. Blocks of DNA define regions called genes, blocks of genes define chromosomes, and interactions between genes and chromosomes affect the final outcome. It is like an instruction book laid out in chapters – another sign of intelligent design.

Furthermore, DNA by itself is not sufficient for life. It needs a mechanism or "machine" to read the code and put it into effect. This DNA machine is simply a biological cell. Simply? How not so. The code that DNA embodies is very complex and organized in itself, but the cell machinery that reads, replicates, and puts it into action is just as complex. This alone should give us a clue that DNA and life as we know it could not have come about by mere random chance.

Even with our great scientific understanding today, we still know very little about how DNA and life in its myriad forms can go from a code into a living, breathing organism, and not just bacteria and plants but every single living thing we see. It is mind boggling how a code and such tiny machinery can produce the great variety of life in existence.

If it were just a matter of mixing up the right compounds in a soup, we would have created our own non-DNA based life forms by now. We would also see alternate forms of non-DNA based life in nature as well. Clearly, there is much more needed to make life work than mixing chemicals.

Let us examine biology closer to see how complex it truly is. The process of cell division (when one cell becomes two) is called mitosis in regular cells or meiosis in sex cells. During cell division, the DNA of the cell is split and copied so that when the cell divides into two, both cells will have a complete copy of the DNA and become two independent but identical cells.

Molecular biologists now know that there is much more at work inside the cell than just the DNA. There is actually tiny machinery at the molecular level that orchestrates and performs the DNA replication process. This biological machinery includes enzymes like topoisomerases that provide critical functions during replication.

Topoisomerases help to relieve the pulling and stretching forces on the DNA strands as they are pulled apart, split, and copied, so that the DNA does not fall apart during replication. They can identify high stress areas in the DNA and then act as a retainer to hold the strands together.

Other enzymes are responsible for the acts of splitting and copying the DNA code. The whole process of cell division is a concerted work of many components, like these enzymes, that when viewed together look exactly like a machine at work on an assembly line. The details of the process are simply astounding.

The atheist attributes this amazing machinery simply to "nature," but the problem is, how can such complex machinery come to exist by mere random chance? The process of DNA replication depends on delicate chemical balances in a controlled environment. Otherwise the enzymes and cellular machinery for replication could not function properly.

The cell itself provides the proper environment for replication to work correctly, so it is as essential to the replication process as the other machinery. The cell wall, the DNA, the enzymes, and all the other components inside the cell work together as a complete machine.

A machine requiring such delicate balances is impossible to come about by pure random chance, not only because randomness cannot provide direction, but also because the chaotic churning of the elements in the natural environment (on our planet and the cosmos) completely negates the possibility of this delicate biochemical machinery coming about by accident.

DNA and the entire workings of life were very cleverly engineered, so well done in fact, that our human capacities are incapable of replicating them from scratch. Perhaps in ten, fifty or one hundred years we may have the knowledge and skills needed to duplicate it? Perhaps, but look at the sheer effort our greatest minds need to put into the task. It tells us that DNA based life is not a lucky, chance invention and I believe that any efforts to reproduce it will only yield limited robotic automatons, not true life as we know it.

We can see now that life depends on a logical and structured code as well as machinery to work with it. This kind of structure I have argued is impossible without direction by an intelligent force. Code and machinery are two things that simply cannot exist without intelligent design behind them. Any engineer can attest to the need for intelligent design when it comes to building code and machines.

You can shake a box of parts forever and they will not assemble themselves into a machine. This is essentially how atheists suggest that DNA based life came into existence, as well as the universe itself, but that would be putting faith in the random variance theory again.

As scientists have studied the origins of life they have found that a certain number of conditions need to be present for complex life, such as ourselves, to exist. This is called the Rare Earth Theory, which states that without a sufficient magnetic field around our planet, a relatively large moon, a stable parent star, long periods of planetary stability, etc., etc, etc, that complex life could not have appeared on our planet. It is a long series of must-haves which points out that we are very lucky to be here, or so it seems.

A Rare Earth is not the only clue to a directed existence. Even the assembly of the elements appear to work in our favor. Consider water, H_2O, which in its liquid form is a critical component for DNA based life. Water is one of very few compounds that expand when cooled (most compounds and elements contract when cooled and expand when heated). This allows ice to float when water freezes and act as an insulating layer so that the water below stays liquid.

It is a critical property of water that enables life to survive changing seasons from temperate summer to frigid winter. If not for this property, lakes, rivers and oceans would freeze completely from top to bottom and kill life before it got the chance to gain a foothold in the environment. Why does water have this rare property that seems tailored to support life? Another lucky fluke? So it seems.

Marks for intelligent influence in our existence now consist of:

1. Infinite random variance is insufficient for creating our universe and DNA based life.
2. The workings of DNA based life are so structured and complex that intelligent design must behind it.
3. Our Rare Earth is very unique.
4. Water and how it behaves is especially well suited for DNA-based life.

It is as if our universe and planet were made for our existence, but hold on, an atheist would bring up the anthropic principle again – that we exist here in this universe and on this planet only because they just happen to be right for life out of all the millions and billions of possible universes and planets. Never mind that I have already argued against alternate universes, but we'll overlook that for the sake of argument. Where else can we find the genius of a creator?

We looked at the smallest structures in life and saw that there are definite signs of intelligent design in them. Let us now look to the current state-of-the-art in physics – superstring theory. True that it is still an unproven theory, but there is now so much evidence for it that physicists believe it is only a matter of time that superstring theory is fully confirmed. The details and mathematics of superstrings are so complex that even the brightest scientists in the world have trouble grasping and working with the theory, so I certainly do not have the capacities to teach or explain it in detail. However, I can note its significance for this discussion.

Superstring theory revolves around the notion of tiny vibrating strings that are the core component for all matter, energy, and force in the universe. There is nothing smaller in superstring theory than these strings, much like letters are the smallest component for words, sentences and paragraphs. The real special thing about these strings is that they are truly like the letters in which everything else can be built from. Nothing more than these strings vibrating at certain frequencies is needed to reproduce every single component of classical physics.

All the subatomic particles that go together to form the atomic components of protons, neutrons and electrons can be made from superstrings. These in turn combine further into larger structures to produce all the elements in the periodic table, such as hydrogen, oxygen, iron, gold, and carbon.

All forms of energy, as well, can be made from superstrings, such as photons for light and other electromagnetic particles like x-rays and gamma rays. Even all the forces of physics, such as magnetism, gravity, and the atomic forces that hold atoms together, can be created out of superstrings.

It is simply amazing that only one structure can recreate everything we know in our physical universe. Well, that is not entirely true, as we will see, but the superstring revolution is exciting to physicists because the force of gravity previously could not be reconciled with the other forces in physics. It had to be treated as a separate entity. The only problem with superstring theory, though, is that it is unproven. There is no experimental confirmation of the theory because we do not have the technical means to probe at the levels needed to confirm it. Yet, physicists hold a great deal of confidence in the theory. Why?

They have a mountain of evidence that supports the theory indirectly. Superstrings work magnificently in logic and formula to reproduce everything in physics. They also give a reasonable explanation for why mass and energy are the same, just as Einstein's famous formula states: $E = MC^2$, Energy equals Mass times the Speed of Light (C) squared. Energy and mass are the same because they both come from the same building block – superstrings.

Superstrings also explain why energy, like light and x-rays, possess the properties of both waves and particles. It was a conundrum in physics. How can a single unit of light (a photon) behave like both a wave and a particle? The answer is, because they are made from superstrings, which are not particles like dots but are vibrating strings. They only seem to be like particles because superstrings are so small.

And then the holy grail of modern physics – unifying gravity with the other forces. Superstrings here too come to the rescue, and so it seems that all of physics can be explained in one complex, but very elegant theory – a "theory of everything."

Very exciting, indeed. However, it isn't about physics that you should be excited about when superstrings are discussed here. We are trying to see reality in its entirety, not just the tangible or testable parts of it. Our Theory of Everything is much broader in scope, but like superstring theory, it also has a mountain of evidence supporting it, and the funny thing is, superstrings are part of that evidence. Superstrings are a profound mark for a creator of physical reality in the same way that DNA is a mark for a creator of life. Why?

Superstring theory and the mechanics of DNA share pure and elegant structure that appear to be designed with a goal in mind because like DNA, superstrings by themselves would be nothing more than a box of inert dust, another box of parts, but when they are set to vibrate at certain frequencies and made to interact with each other through the mediums of further laws, space and time, it all works together like a grand machine – structure upon structure upon structure – impossible to exist as I have argued using theories of infinite random variance.

One could argue, though, that a creator for DNA based life could have been some ancient alien life form that has since died off or is unknown to us, but you cannot argue away the fabric of the universe in such a way. The creator of the universe necessarily must be outside of that universe. However, the similarities in the pure genius of DNA based life and the structure of our universe based on superstrings point to a very similar intelligence – one that is far beyond what we can imagine – and so similar in fact that it points to the same origin for both.

The proof is in the structure of life as well as physical reality. They both boil down to singular, very elegantly constructed entities (DNA and superstrings) that when put into operation produce so much more than the sum of their parts. One becomes many on an order of magnitude beyond imagination, like the letters, words and sentences of language can combine to create an infinite variety of communication.

DNA has its machinery that is needed for it to work and superstrings has its machinery (the laws governing their operation). These things go together and are so complex and structured, yet so elegantly designed, that intelligent design must necessarily be behind them, just as the writer is behind the story and the artist is behind the portrait. How else can the parameters of superstrings be set properly to create everything we see in the universe, including specifications that are perfect for DNA based life, when infinite random variance or random anything is inadequate to explain it?

Scientists must have reasonable alternative theories that could support the existence of our reality and life with absolutely zero intelligent influence, but there are currently no theories that do not involve the theoretical notions of infinite random variance – the simple mixing of a soup whether it be a cosmic soup for the universe or a primordial organic soup for life.

To make progress, one needs to look to a more plausible explanation – an explanation that not only has back up from a variety of sources but also melds physical reality with life in such a way that it becomes obvious that everything in existence belongs under one umbrella. The explanation I bring forward now is that there is a creator and not just any creator but the one we know as God – the final solidifying agent we need to fully draft reality.

Not Just Any God

When I speak of God, I refer to the only one who fits as the foundation for all creation – our universe, biological life, and our own existence. How can I make this assertion when there are many gods in many religions with many creation stories? Am I simply being prejudiced or conceited in my thinking? You will see in the next chapter how I stand on that question.

For now, I speak based on what I have learned during this "drafting up" of reality, which is through the thousands of years of human history, there is only one god who has proven himself to believers time and again with miracles, prophecies that have come, facts and details about history, spirituality, human nature and even science that are backed up from sources outside the Bible. This is the one and only true God – he who is called Yahweh in the Old Testament and is the God of Israel as well as all Christians today.

Consider how I just mentioned that both life and the fabric of the universe can be shown to come from the same source, the same Creator. Not only are their designs similar and ingeniously elegant, but they both share a component of reality that, though, has not been scientifically confirmed, nonetheless exists – a spiritual component. Some people think that anything spiritual is nonsense and imaginary hocus pocus, but that would not be the right line of thought to expand understanding of reality. Conclusions of this sort would be falling to Selective Reasoning.

The spiritual side of nature is simply a part of it that is invisible, yes, but is as ingrained in all life and reality and as essential to them as your blood is to your own livelihood. The spiritual side of nature is just another aspect of reality – one that is not easy or may actually be impossible to probe with the scientific method.

Accepting a spiritual side to ourselves and life is straightforward since most of us have been exposed to ideas of the human spiritual world with life after death, meditation, and life energy or chi and other spiritual notions, but a spiritual side to physical reality itself is harder to grasp.

The Bible alludes to this spiritual part of the natural world in passages like Leviticus 18:25 *"Even the land was defiled; so I punished it for its sin, and the land vomited out its inhabitants,"* and other instances of "the land" becoming contaminated or saturated with sin or "bad energy." Are these references simply narrative tools or more literal?

To answer this, look at another aspect of the spiritual realm – hauntings. There are two types of hauntings. The first are what we generally think of as a haunting, which deal with the interactions of ghosts, spirits or other invisible, intelligent beings with people, but the other kind are more like a geographic recording in which a particular location seems to play back over and over again an intense event in its history, such as the sounds and events of a long gone battle can sometimes be heard and seen in some old fields of war. These types of hauntings are not interactive or "intelligent" but simply seem to be a recording of space-time at that location.

The spiritual side of reality can also be experienced with psychics who can "read" an object or location simply by being there or touching it. These abilities have been used to good effect by law enforcement seeking information about a crime that only a direct witness could know.

These aspects of physical reality point to a spiritual component that has something in common with the spiritual part of ourselves and life in general. Perhaps calling this aspect of reality "spiritual" is confusing since we tend to associate spiritual things with notions of being alive. In this context, I only want to convey that physical reality has a scientifically unknown component that operates in a way we do not understand and that we and life in general also have similar components that are not understood by science.

Indeed, I believe that all of Creation, our physical reality and life, are tied together by a common "spiritual" component and this common ground between them is another link that tells us there is one creator for all of it.

Circling Evidence in the Bible

One creator, but again, why the god of Israel and Christianity? Inevitably, when we talk about God we must also talk about the Bible and God's Word. Its content and validity has been disputed throughout the centuries, but through every attack it has stood intact almost unchanged since the earliest writings thousands of years ago. The Bible remains solid because its foundation is solid.

There are many works by other authors and experts about the validity of the Bible and its contents, so I will not repeat their insights here. Anyone interested in studying this aspect of the Bible should read Lee Strobel's book, *A Case For Christ*, and the works of the experts that he consults as a good starting point for studying how valid and true the Bible really is. My contribution here is to build on those other works and note that science has actually validated many things in the Bible that were thought to be untrue or too preposterous to even consider as true.

As crazy or implausible as some of the content in the Bible seems, much of it has been confirmed through research and other scientific discoveries through the years. I will note some of the more recent discoveries. Consider the Adam and Eve story in which all humans are said to be descended from these two people.

There is actually scientific evidence of this in the Mitochondrial Eve theory where it was found that every human today has one and only one common maternal ancestor – an Eve. This intriguing evidence was found through the study of mitochondrial DNA (mtDNA), a type of DNA that is inherited only from the mother.

mtDNA was examined from populations around the world and it was found that commonalities for all populations made a geographic trail leading back to one geographic source and one maternal ancestor. The mtDNA geographic trail also matches anthropological and archeological evidence that had already been studied showing the migration of the human population through its earliest history – a trail that leads to one location somewhere in the northeast African region. Coincidence? That is a question I will bring up many times here.

Perhaps it is a coincidence these separate fields of science match up and tell the same story. It may also be a coincidence that there even is a Mitochondrial Eve – that there is only one maternal ancestor for all of us. But science says it is possible that Eve would have had contemporaries living at the same time as her. It is only that the family lines of Eve's contemporaries either completely died off or a generation had only sons to further the line and so the mtDNA for that maternal line was lost. This theoretical possibility leaves doubt to the Eve known in the Bible, but there are many more validations of the Bible than through DNA evidence.

How about another Biblical story, The Great Flood, in which the whole of the earth was flooded with rain for 40 days. There is scientific evidence for this too in the fossil record and sedimentary soil samples around the world that points to a very swift (in geologic terms) and massive flow of fresh water everywhere. Coincidence? Is it also coincidence that almost all cultures from around the world have a Great Flood story that are so similar that a common root must be considered?

The last two examples of Biblical evidence had to do with scientific confirmations. There is much more evidence if you look into the work of other people, as I have mentioned. It ranges from historical documentation in non-Biblical sources to archeological finds that confirm Biblical content and further confirmations from other areas of the sciences. Another good reference for more scientific validation of Bible content is Ray Comfort's book, *Scientific Facts in the Bible.* Can so much logical and scientific validation of the Bible all be mere coincidence?

How about this last piece of scientific evidence? It concerns the notion of a global consciousness – that all of us are linked somehow to each other and the universe as a whole. There is an ongoing academic study called the Global Consciousness Project or EGG, which has found correlations in apparently random data that coincide with major events around the world.

The study monitors dozens of physical random number generators (machines that produce random numbers without human intervention) around the world, and it has found through statistical analysis of the results that spikes in the data come just before major events such as the terrorist attacks on September 11th, 2001, bombings and other terrorist attacks, economic crisis, large earthquakes, major accidents like plane crashes, and even Christmas Eve.

This amazing correlation suggests a link between the very workings of the universe with our own nature and what is important to us as humans. This is yet another tick mark for that common "spiritual" component that I argue is further proof that everything in existence comes from one source – one Creator.

How else can machines that simply output random numbers correlate so strongly with totally unrelated events that are only important as it relates to us and our lives if there is not an actual connection between the fabrics of the universe and our own being? Science cannot explain this, but the Bible can and does. Both the universe and ourselves owe existence to one common source.

When you look at all the correlating evidence for Biblical validity it begins to stack up, higher and higher, such that it cannot be ignored any longer. A logical person would have to come to the conclusion that if there is so much real world validation of things in the Bible then it would be reasonable to assume that much more of its content is valid and true, even the things about the so-called imaginary and intangible, like angels, spirituality, and creation.

This logic is no different than scientists assuming that superstring theory is true. It too is just as unproven and unconfirmed as God and the spiritual world, but there is so much evidence for it that the probability of it being true soars to near 100%. Anyone who overlooks the evidence for Biblical validity yet believes in the evidence for superstring theory would be falling to Selective Reasoning. We cannot fall to such fallacies of reasoning if we are to understand reality in its entirety.

The Blind Can See

We are just as the blind using sticks to poke about our reality in order to understand it, but our sticks are not the best means for getting a true picture of reality – that blueprint we are after. How then can the blind see? It is only through someone who can see and understand that we may see. That someone only need tell us through language and concepts that we can understand for us to gain the insights we need to view reality in its truest form.

"Meaningless! Meaningless!" says the Teacher. "Utterly meaningless! Everything is meaningless." Ecclestiastes 1:2. The Teacher, for us is God, the only person to have proven his knowledge to be valid and true in so many ways, not just through the Bible but also externally by science and other sources. The quote from Ecclestiastes is a very simple statement but it can only be understood in context.

Why is everything, all **human** wisdom, knowledge and work, meaningless? Recall the Superlative Data Blob I brought up earlier. It is an impressive collection of knowledge, but in the end it is a meaningless mass because it does nothing to show purpose – the meaning behind our existence and everything else.

It is only when the Teacher sheds light onto that purpose and answers the why and how we are here that the Blob can solidify into a clear picture of reality. In other words, it is only when reality is framed by God that we may see it true. Life, existence, and reality itself gain that meaning that was absent in the knowledge gained from the chaotic churning of poking mere sticks.

To show that God is truly the solidifying factor for our reality, I will now move on to the last and probably the most interesting source of validation and evidence for Him and His Word in the Bible. This source is what a large part of the content in the Bible is composed of – witness testimony.

Why else are the major sections of the Bible called the Old and New **Testaments**? It is through witness testimony that many things are proven true to those who did not witness directly. We see this working in the courts of law every day and to discount it in this context would be another act of Selective Reasoning.

Atheists would like to dismiss witness testimony entirely because it cannot be explained other than to brand the witnesses incapable, insane, or liars, but this tact would be illogical because of the sheer amount of witness testimony we have today and throughout history. You may be able to dismiss a handful of cases but hundreds and thousands, if not millions, all over the world, today and through many centuries?

A simple look at statistics will immediately tell you that not all witnesses are incapable or insane or lying. Certainly some people may be crazy or lying or just mistaken but 100 percent? 50 percent? Even 20% is too large a percentage to brand the general population as invalid or too unreasonable to believe. The numbers simply do not support dismissal on that order.

In fact, witness testimony is probably the most valid of all evidence because through it and the witnesses themselves we can share in their perspective and gain their insights from having experienced reality in ways we have not. The next two chapters will give the testimony of two witnesses, myself and Bill Wilson, who I introduced in Chapter One with a recounting of one of his amazing experiences. Our testimony will serve here to further highlight the true blueprint of reality and show that not only is there a God, but another who has been appointed as the Teacher, Gatekeeper, and Guide for all of humanity.

3rd Compass

Encompassing All

"I am the light of the world. Whoever follows me will never walk in darkness, but will have the light of life." John 8:12

*T*he person quoted above is the Light who can illuminate our life maps and guide us along that ideal path I spoke of in Chapter One. This entire chapter will lay out my journey to discovering this person. Most believers already know who I speak of, but for the rest it may be as much a mystery as it was for me, so I hope that reading my journey will be as much a revelation to you as it was to me. My testimony is compiled from journal entries, memory, and other written correspondence and is as true and accurate as I can make it.

I will start by describing myself and my background. I am a French-Vietnamese American who came to the United States as a refugee of the Vietnam War in 1975. I was two and a half years old at the time and settled into the Minneapolis/St. Paul (Twin Cities) area of Minnesota with my mother and younger sister. Ties to my father and the rest of our family were broken during the quick evacuation and resettlement, so I grew up with a small family in the urban areas of St. Paul.

The large part of my religious exposure as I grew up was that I had none. My mother calls herself a Buddhist, but she never taught us anything religious, rituals, or even brought up the topic of god. She believes all that is necessary for a person to be right with the world is to simply be as good a person as one can be – having a kind heart towards others, never harming anyone, and not breaking "the rules," such as stealing, lying and so on.

This value system was instilled in me and I kept it into my adult life. I believed, as many people do in this day, that it is not necessary to do anything more to be a good person than to simply have good intentions and not harm anyone in my actions. It made perfect sense to me while notions of going to church and adhering to the rules and regulations of religion did not.

Church and religion in general felt too ritualized and stringent to me. I grew up being exposed to the American ideals of independence and free will. Those values too became ingrained in me and fueled the rebel inside. I often spent time as a loner and did my own thing, my way. "My way" could very well be the motto for today's America as well as Western society as a whole. These values don't mix well with church and religion, so I stayed away from them.

The only times I had gone to church were for a funeral and a couple times when my mother brought us to some services at the suggestion of family friends who were part of the Catholic community that helped sponsor our family's relocation. I only recall of the experiences that it was very boring and I did not understand anything going on or being said. A typical response for a preteen child who had not been taught any Christian material.

The other part of my exposure to religious notions came from the mass media. My family celebrated Christmas, but it was a family holiday mainly for giving gifts and being together to us. Any connection to Christianity was overlooked. You could say we simply assimilated the culture and bought into the commercialism of the holidays without concerning ourselves with the historical or religious meanings.

It was the same thing for Easter. That was just a spring festival to me just as Halloween was the fall festival. All I cared about as a kid was that we got to eat a lot of candy during these times and Christmas was real special because of the gifts and sparkling evergreen trees.

Yes, especially the gifts – toy robots, Lego sets, cars, trucks and army men – made the boy jump for joy, but I did also learn about the "Christmas spirit" through stories like *A Christmas Carol, Rudolph the Red Nosed Reindeer, The Grinch Who Stole Christmas*, and *It's a Good Life*. Anyone can pick up the Christmas spirit through the media and by observing people during the holidays, but there is something missing about this watered down, commercialized version of the holidays that I would not discover until much later in life.

Besides having a small family and being a first generation immigrant, my upbringing was very typical urban, Midwest American. I was a good kid for the most part, made good grades, liked to play sports on occasion, but mainly I was a geek during my teenage years. My step-father, whom my mother married about four years into our relocation, had bought me one of the first home computers of the era (a Commodore 64) when I was 12 years old.

Playing video games was fun, but another aspect of the computer era really caught my attention as I learned that computers could be made to do many interesting things just by telling them to. Well, not exactly by telling them, but by writing instructions for them to follow. For a kid who was always told what to do, this was a very satisfying and empowering thing. I had been initiated into computer programming, which would eventually become a large part of my future.

After high school, I went to the University of Minnesota Institute of Technology under an architectural program. I had become a very proficient computer programmer by then and considered a computer science degree, but I also had a creative side that I wanted to explore. Writing, drawing, and painting had always been things I enjoyed, but I knew that a career in these fields would be uncertain. Everyone has heard of the starving artists. Well, starving was a career option I did not want to participate in, so I mixed some creativity in my career path and tried out architecture.

I learned, though, that the profile of an architect did not fit my personality. It was not just about drawing, designing, and engineering but also about people skills and marketing to sell your designs. I knew my mediocre designs would not sell themselves and I am an absolutely horrible sales person, so I jumped over to what I knew best. I switched to a computer science program that emphasized computer graphics, systems design, and artificial intelligence.

It was a very science and engineering oriented program with years of calculus, physics, and psychology. My grades were very good and I was set to succeed, but I also had problems. I had been going to college partly on an academic scholarship, but that ran out after four years. I had also been working part-time to pay for the rest, but when my scholarship money was gone I started to struggle with paying for college. I had to drop classes, become a part-time student and work more hours.

Two more years passed of trying to work a job and going to college, but it wore on me and after reviewing my progress, I figured out I had at least another two years to go. Finishing college now felt like scaling a vertical cliff a hundred stories high. My spirit sunk just looking at the goal. I was ready to quit. I had already secured a good computer job with my skills, so I figured I could just keep that job and leave college.

My ultimate goal was to have my own business anyways since my independent nature tended to want things "My Way." I thought, why do I need a piece of paper from some place saying I am qualified when I can prove myself? Actions speak louder than words, after all. The more I thought about it, the easier it became, and the rebel in me begged to leave the academic life, so after more than six years I left college to begin the next chapter of my life.

After college I led a typical adult life – worked full-time at a good paying, stable job and spent the rest of the time pursuing my other goals, which were mainly to have my own successful business and have a family.

Over ten years passed since I left college. I had gotten married, had a son, mortgage, and stayed at the same job through it all. I thought my life was very typical suburban American. That is, until 2005 when I got the first clue that there would be big changes ahead.

Signal Ahead

Sunday, July 17th, 2005 – I woke earlier than usual and as I lay in bed, I noticed on the floor there was a ring of light centered perfectly around one of the roller feet of the office chair next to the bed. I thought that was peculiar, so I sat up and pushed the chair away to see the ring of light better. When I did this, it revealed the ring to be a ticking clock composed of several short, evenly spaced lines around the circumference just like the markings on an analog clock. There was also another small line that moved as a seconds hand, ticking off the time. The whole image was about three inches in diameter and it shown a brilliant yellow like sunlight.

Perplexed, I looked around the bedroom wondering what could be making this detailed projection on the floor. The curtain on the only window in the room was drawn and there were only a few slivers of bright light shining around the edges. There were no other light sources in the room, so I got up and waved my hand above and around the shining clock to try and find the source of the projection. Nothing I did disturbed the image.

Then I placed my hand directly over the clock and the image shown on my hand and followed its contours just as if a projector was aimed at my hand. This meant the image was being projected right out of the air surrounding it! I thought, "Wow, that is weird," but I couldn't explain it and I was sleepy, so I laid back in bed for some time thinking about it. After some minutes, I looked back at the floor and the image was gone while nothing else in the room had changed. It must be a sign or message of some kind, I thought, but what and from who? Maybe I was running out of time for something, but I did not feel a sense of urgency from it. I thought it must be important, though, so I wrote about it in my journal.

Another three years passed by as I continued life and more or less forgot about the ticking clock. I was mainly trying to accomplish my goal of being successful on my own, working in all my spare time trying different avenues that would use my more creative skills, such as graphic design, art and writing. The freelance work in desktop publishing, graphic design, painting, and Internet design was always sporadic though, and the need to do the work in my spare time made it difficult. Success never materialized and through the years all the time I spent on it put a burden on my family life and my marriage became strained as I kept trying to free myself of the 9 to 5 job.

Sometimes when it was quiet, I contemplated my direction in life, and I remembered the clock of sunlight. I kept pondering what it could mean. It was real, almost tangible. The experience left a vivid memory of it in my mind. Am I running out of time? Is the world running out of time? I wanted to figure it out, so I consulted a friend who knew more about spiritual things and symbolism.

She thought that since the vision came in the morning it meant a beginning, not end, and that sunlight is a sign of prosperity and richness, so that was also a good thing. She thought that the clock meant I should slow down my life, stop trying so hard to work on so many things at once, and enjoy the richness of family and life more – simplify. At the time, that interpretation made sense to me. I needed to slow down and enjoy life more.

Signs Ahead

I believe I did tone down my search for success and independence after that... for a few weeks, anyways. How easy it is to be told something, take it to heart, and then some days later simply forget about it. My passion for being independent kept eating at me, and I continued working at all hours and creating stress for myself and my family. It finally caught up with me on Sunday, April 27th, 2008 when I needed to go to the health clinic for a painful rash I believe was stress related.

I thought it would be another typical long wait at the doctor's office, but while I waited I noticed something strange on the violet, velvety felt seat cushions of the chairs directly in front of me. There were two women sitting across from me in those chairs just before and when they left, I saw distinct images on the seat cushions that caught my eye. The images were formed by dark and light shades of the felt fabric. You know how when you brush a thick carpet one way or the other and the direction that the fibers are brushed will change the pattern of the fibers in a way to create a different shade of the fabric's color? The images on these seat cushions were made in this way.

The image on the left was of a fox, curled up around itself like it was sleeping. The head, body and tail were clearly defined so there was no mistaking the image. The image on the other chair was even more detailed. It showed the face of a monkey, like a chimpanzee, and there was a round analog clock in its left ear, which seemed to point to 9:10. I thought, another clock. Could this be related to the clock I saw three years ago?

I sat and stared at the images for a good half hour while I waited to be called. How could these well formed images be on two different chairs that just had people sitting on them? They looked like an artist took a small brush to the fabric and painted the images there. I looked at the dozen other chairs around me and none of them had images like these two. They only had random blotches of light and dark in the felt, exactly what you would expect to see on these cushions. The images had to be another message for me like the clock of sunlight, so I tried to interpret them.

The fox was easy. I thought it referred to my son whose name, Todd, means fox, and because the image was on a soft, violet purple background, which conveys calm and comfort, I interpreted it as, "Find comfort in my son." I needed to spend more time with my son. That made sense to me. I had been neglecting a lot of family time.

Then I turned to the monkey and also thought it might stand for a person, but I had no idea who it could refer to. And then the clock pointing to 9:10, I did not understand what it could mean either, so like the clock of sunlight, I jotted down these "visions" or "signs" in my journal and went about my life.

A Revelation

Fast forward five months to Sunday, October 19th, 2008 – My wife had started hanging out with a new friend, Natalie, from work some time during the summer, and she often described her as fast paced, always running around, and talking very quickly. On this day, my wife mentioned these attributes again, also saying that she was just like a monkey. A switch clicked in my mind and the fox and monkey vision came back to me.

I thought, "Wait, is there more to this person?" So I thought about that clock pointing to 9:10 and pondered, maybe it stood for the time I met Natalie. I had not written about meeting her in my journal since I did not write in it regularly, so I dated our meeting indirectly. I went back to some digital photographs that I knew were dated about

10 days after I met her. They were dated September 20th. Subtract 10 days and we have September 10th, 9/10 or 9:10 on the clock. Coincidence?

Now my interest was peaked and on a hunch, I had to confirm something else and ask Natalie what year she was born because on the Chinese Zodiak, animals represent certain years on a 12 year cycle. I was born in 1972, the Year of the Rat. I had to find out if she was born on a Year of the Monkey.

Of course, asking this question of someone I am only an acquaintance is out of the ordinary, and after she confirmed to me that, yes, she was born in a Year of the Monkey, she asked what it was all about. I did not want to tell her everything out of fear of looking like a lunatic talking about visions and signs, but I knew if they prophesied meeting her then it meant something important, and she would have to know the whole story.

I told her about the visions and signs and wondered what her response would be. Would she just brand me crazy? Well, her response was more simple than I thought – God – and then I was the one to take a step back.

What? I thought. Of course she would say that since I knew she was a devoted Christian, but what does God have to do with this? I recoiled from notions of Christianity, God, and religion because I had grown up thinking they were just ways for conformers and goodie-goodies to spend time. The whole idea of going to church and praying before an invisible spirit did not make sense to a very independent and scientifically minded person like me.

Then I thought about it more. I was given a prophesy that foretold months in advance I would meet a person fitting a certain description, at a certain time, and furthermore, whose name means Christmas Day (Natalie comes from Natalia, which means Christmas

Day from the Latin natale domini) and who also said that she had been praying to let God use her to help people who were searching for or needed Him.

There were too many details lining up now and the simple fact that I was told it would happen far in advance through a prophetic sign sent chills down my spine. If I were not to follow this through, it would be like throwing away a winning lottery ticket, so I let Natalie get me a couple books from the library about Christianity.

I started with Max Lucado's book, *Just Like Jesus,* and only a quarter of the way through reading it, everything clicked – the signs, my life, everything synched. I asked Natalie how and why she picked that book because it had exactly the message I needed to understand. She said the only reason she picked it was that she recognized the author. She never read it before and was in a hurry, so she just grabbed it.

Her hand must have been guided because the main message in the book was that God wants us all to be more like Jesus. This message might not jar anything in just anyone, but for me it highlighted some very strange "coincidences" concerning myself, like one of my favorite numbers is 3, 30, 33 or any number with threes. Three is also an important number in the Bible concerning Christ. There were 3 wise men that visited the new born Jesus. Jesus was baptized and started his ministry at 30, which went on for 3 years. Jesus was 33 years old when he was crucified. He was resurrected 3 days afterward and he appeared to the disciples 3 times after his resurrection.

I had no idea why I liked the number three. It just "felt right," and now it synched with Christ. Seven is my other favorite number and also important in the Bible, meaning wholeness, but that one is more understandable since it commonly also stands for luck to most people.

Another big "coincidence" was the artwork on my motorcycle, which I had painted in 2004 before any of the visions and signs. The main theme on the tank mural was a crusader's shield with a cross and a dragon breathing fire on it (see photo at right).

At the time, I simply thought I would like my bike to have a medieval armor theme and the crusader's cross was the first

My 2004 motorcycle tank mural
(see Insert 2 for color photo)

thing that came to mind. It also had to have a dragon because, well, everybody loves dragons. Dragons to me were like dinosaurs to a 5 year old boy. They were grand and awe inspiring beasts.

Little did I know the Christian symbolism in that airbrushed mural – a dragon attacking the cross. To a Christian it symbolizes Satan or Sin attacking Christ or Christianity, and in my mural the dragon's fire is repelled by the shield and cross, which would symbolize Christ triumphing over evil. Now that is an unusually Christian message for a very un-Christian artist who was just painting things that filled his fancy. Coincidence again?

Another thing that clinched my "lottery ticket" was my name, which I had changed in 2004 because my step-father had adopted me when I was a teen. During that process my name was changed to a more American one and I took his surname. Through the years though, my mother and step-father separated and I wanted to change my surname back to my birth name. When I pondered the name change, I also did not want to go completely back to my given first and middle names, which I did not like, so I chose Ty, short for Tyrone. Ty was my familiar name, like a nickname, that my family had always called me, and for my middle name I chose Alexander because I wanted it to match the middle name we had given our son.

What does this naming have to do with Jesus? The funny thing is, Tyrone is a Greek name meaning sovereign and Alexander is another Greek name meaning savior. Put them together and it is Sovereign Savior. If I wasn't influenced by some unseen force telling me to be like Jesus, our **Sovereign** Lord and **Savior**, then this would be another amazing coincidence.

There were more coincidental things about my life and preferences that matched up with Christian ideals and teachings. I just could not explain it. How could there be so many of these coincidences when I was not a Christian or had Christian friends? I had even recoiled from Christian and other religious institutions in my life. It was baffling to me. That lotto ticket was not just matching three or four numbers but every single one plus the bonus boxes.

I thought it was impossible, yet all the matching numbers stared back at me. I kept thinking, maybe it was all a strange coincidence, but there comes a tipping point when mere circumstantial evidence accumulates so much that it turns into solid, irrefutable proof.

Denying that evidence would be like a jury acquitting a murderer because his finger prints or DNA were not on the murder weapon or at the crime scene, but a stack of other evidence pointed directly at his involvement in the murder, such as his shoe print on the blood stained floor and his clothes fibers on the victim's body.

I also considered how I was brought to this stage – by two visions separated by years, but both occurring on a Sunday – the Lord's day – and one of them was a prophetic vision that had made abstract symbols materialize right into life. That in itself was amazing, but all the rest on top made me understand completely. I had interpreted the fox on purple velvet as, "Find comfort in my son," but now I knew it should be, "Find comfort in **My Son**," where "My Son" refers to God's son, Jesus Christ. Furthermore, not only does purple stand for comfort, but very appropriate in this context is that purple is also the color for royalty, as well as the color of Jesus' robe during his crucifixion.

The soldiers twisted together a crown of thorns and put it on his head. They clothed him in a purple robe and went up to him again and again saying, "Hail, king of the Jews!" John 19:2

Clearly, the symbolism in the fox and monkey visions were multi-layered and very elegant, showing a mastery of communication that I only wish I could achieve. The clock of sunlight was also elegant, but its meaning was more ambiguous. I now believe it said that a time of spiritual prosperity and fulfillment was coming – a time for the Lord to come. All of this was amazing and inspiring, but it was actually just the beginning.

When I had told friends of my experience – about cashing in the lottery ticket and following Christ – Bill Wilson, our second witness, congratulated me and said that I would be embarking on an amazing journey.

I did not quite know what he meant, but now I understand completely. The point when I realized Jesus was behind not just the visions that led to Him, but also behind the fabric of my own being was an epiphany – a revelation – and everything else after that was truly and profoundly life changing.

Guided by the Light

"If anyone is thirsty, let him come to me and drink. Whoever believes in me, as the Scripture has said, streams of living water will flow from within him." John 7:37

I believed. The evidence that Jesus Christ was real and working in my life was put before me, and it was so overwhelming and convincing that I felt like the apostle Paul, who, a former unbeliever and persecutor of Christians, was turned into a believer by the resurrected Jesus and set on a new path after being overwhelmingly convinced as well.

Jesus had appeared to Paul in a brilliant flash of light, spoke to him, and blinded him – an experience a bit more overwhelming than mine – so I am grateful I was only given a trail of signs to follow. The result was the same, though. Our lives were turned around and we were pointed to a new direction – the 3rd Compass now guided us.

The passage in John 7 above speaks of "living water." This refers to the Holy Spirit, which is a component of God just as Christ is. I like to think of the Holy Spirit as the means by which we are connected to God (and in conjunction, Christ, and everyone else as well). It is God's energy and presence in us – flowing within us – and through the Spirit, God may guide us more directly through "spiritual gifts."

Now to each [person] the manifestation of the Spirit is given for the common good. To one there is given through the Spirit the message of wisdom, to another the message of knowledge by means of the same Spirit, to another faith by the same Spirit, to another gifts of healing by that one Spirit, to another miraculous powers, to another prophecy, to another

distinguishing between spirits, to another speaking in different kinds of tongues, and to still another the interpretation of tongues. All these are the work of one and the same Spirit, and he gives them to each one, just as he determines.
1 Corinthians 12:7

When I began to step forward, to quench my spiritual thirst and drink, I noticed some unusual things happening when I was praying and especially when praying for guidance. I started to get visions, but this time they were the traditional kind that are manifested inside the mind.

I began to see coherent and fluid images in my mind as I closed my eyes and prayed. This had never happened before during meditation, which I was familiar with, or at any other times in my life. Normally, when I close my eyes I just see darkness and maybe splotches of light here or there. Never had I seen any well formed images.

At first they seemed random and I could not understand their meaning, but then things started popping up in real life some time afterwards, hours or days, that exactly matched what I saw in my mind. I originally thought, are these coincidences? But many times this happened.

The first ones appeared inconsequential, such as I would see an uncommon and distinct object in my mind and a short time later I would see it in life, like I had seen the Eiffel Tower in vision and then the next day while shopping at a store I came across a small model of the Eiffel.

Some people suggested that I may have developed a mental illness or a brain tumor that caused the visions, but the circumstances made these explanations silly. Would someone all of a sudden go insane or form a tumor because they started praying to Jesus? I had only gotten these visions while I was praying as well. Any kind of illness would manifest at all other times.

After a few weeks, the visions became more focused on telling me a message, such as guidance to tell me something that was happening at the moment or soon after. I started to put the experiences together and figured out that not only was I being guided by these visions, but I was also given the gift of prophecy – things I saw in my mind started to materialize in the real world, just like the fox and monkey visions did.

Other examples of this guidance occurred on Christmas Eve 2008. I received visions of wedding bells, which I did not understand, but some days later a friend of mine told me that she and her sister were both asked to be married on Christmas Eve at the same time. The same night, I also received visions of a knight in full armor standing with a sword pointing down straight into the ground, and it had long, straight hand guards so that it resembled a cross. The knight looked strong and resolute, and I interpreted the vision at the time to mean: have strength and resolve in conflict, to stand my ground.

Later I learned that the vision reflects a concept in the Bible about "The Armor of God," which I was unaware at the time. When I examined the vision more closely, the knight was standing strong and resolute which parallels, *"Therefore put on the full armor of God, so that when the day of evil comes, you may be able to stand your ground"* Ephesians 6:9.

The knight also stood behind the sword resembling a cross, stating that the knight wields the cross and is also protected by it. It is a symbol of His Spirit, which parallels another part of God's armor *"the sword of the Spirit, which is the word of God."* Ephesians 6:17. This was one of the first visions I had that gave me Christian or

Biblical concepts before I learned about them or read about it in the Bible.

Another instance of this "teaching through vision" happened on March 3, 2009 when I had a vision of a Maltese Cross, but it was different from the Maltese Crosses I was familiar with. They usually have broad arms and slightly rounded lines – the type of cross on the Red Baron's airplane and those that many motorcyclists like to bare as a standard.

The "familiar" Maltese Cross

The cross I saw was different, very straight and pointy, and when I looked up the Maltese Cross later, I found that the cross I saw in my vision matched exactly the "true" Maltese Cross, which is the symbol of the Knights of Malta or Knights Hospitaller,

The Maltese Cross seen in vision

also known as the Sovereign Military Hospitaller Order of Knights of St. John of Jerusalem – clearly a Christian symbol. I had no idea the Maltese Cross had Christian origins, thinking mainly that it was German because I had associated it with the Red Baron and World War II.

The visions were not the only miraculous gift I was graced with during prayer. The Holy Spirit also guided my hands when I opened my Bible for prayer. It is an uncanny ability to go directly to passages in the Bible that pertain to what is going on at the time. This gift I discovered like the visions, through repeated "coincidences" that kept occurring until I connected the dots with comprehension. It started because it was suggested that I have an open Bible when I prayed, but I had no idea where it should be opened to, so I simply asked the Lord to guide me and open my Bible.

I did not think anything of it at first. The first time I suspected something was going on was when my Bible opened to a passage that had just been brought up at a sermon in church earlier. It was a part of the New Testament, but I thought, well, it could just be a coincidence since the New Testament contains the most common preaching material. Then these coincidences kept happening over time, and one of them that surprised me was on Monday, January 19, 2009, the day after the pastor at my church had talked about King Josiah finding the lost Book of the Law of the Lord.

Pastor Rob had said this story was in Kings, but this morning my Bible opened to 2 Chronicles 34:12 where only one paragraph later the section titled "The Book of the Law Found" began. I thought, wait, this is what Pastor Rob was talking about yesterday, but it's in 2 Chronicles. I thought maybe Pastor Rob was mistaken, but some time later when I had read Kings I saw that the story about King Josiah was there as well. Another amazing coincidence?

Again like the signs and visions, there were too many "coincidences" to discount and I started accepting that God was communicating to me through His Word in the Bible to speak to me and guide me, as well as to go with and reinforce the visions I got. In the case of these passages about King Josiah, I believe God was saying I should take to heart Pastor Rob's sermon about changing my life and myself before I had to or was forced to because of some kind of emergency, like a heart attack or personal crisis, just as King Josiah did when he found the Book of the Law.

Another example of my direct Bible guidance was on January 30, 2009 when I was having a debate about religion on an Internet forum. This forum is an international group of motorcyclists where I had made many friends during the last four years. I had shared with them my experience in finding Christ through the visions and

"Miss Christmas Day," and we were having a heated debate about interpretations and Christianity.

At lunch I decided to ask the Lord for guidance in the debate and I was directed to Acts 2:19, right in the middle of a passage where the apostle Peter is quoting the prophet Joel:

In the last days, God says, I will pour out my Spirit on all people. **Your sons and daughters will prophesy, your young men and women will see visions**, *your old men will dream dreams. Even on my servants, both men and women,*

I will pour out my Spirit in those days, and they will prophesy. I will show wonders in the heaven above and signs on the earth below, blood and fire and bellows of smoke. *The sun will be turned to darkness and the moon to blood before the coming of the great and glorious day of the Lord. And everyone who calls on the name of the Lord will be saved.*
Acts 2:17

I quoted that passage when the debate continued and bolded the text as I did above to highlight what was happening with me as well as around the world. I also told them that I was guided directly to this passage without doing any kind of index search or anything else. Of course, these details were ignored by the skeptics, but I would likely do the same if I were in their shoes. It sounds too crazy to be true. This passage about "The Last Days" is an interesting one, but right now I will continue with my personal testimony. I will come back to it in the last chapter of this book.

The combined Bible guidance and visions over a period of months were proving to me again and again that there wasn't a problem with me, such as going insane or simply trying to make mere coincidences meaningful when they shouldn't be. There were far too many instances of external corroboration in the real world with my guidance. It had begun to steer me on my life map along the ideal path that would lead me to my ultimate and proper place in life. But not only this, the guidance was also teaching me to understand Biblical concepts and reality as a whole in the framework it was intended to be understood. Not through science but through God.

It appeared that I was being taught as a disciple of Christ by the Teacher himself. I certainly know how that statement sounds. It marks me suffering with some form of dementia or schizophrenia and having delusions of grandeur. Some people suggested this to me, but I know I am no one special or insane. There are times when I sound prideful and arrogant because I often speak with confidence, but these are not from delusions of grandeur. It is only because I know my abilities and am confident in them.

There is quite a difference between confidence and arrogance and even more so between those and delusions of grandeur. If I proclaimed myself Jesus Christ himself, then there would be valid grounds to call me delusional, but the simple truth is, I am no better and have no special abilities beyond anyone else. In fact, I can think of much better writers and ministers who could write this book, but something that God wants for all of us is to find their proper place in life. How that happens will be discussed more in Chapter Six, but here I will continue to relay my personal journey.

My guidance led me on March 10, 2009 to Zechariah 3 and 4, which suggested to me that like Joshua, the high priest, I was also a stick snatched from the fire and chosen to help minister God's Word. On March 24, 2009 this message was reinforced when my guidance led me to 1 Peter 2 about *"The Living Stone and a Chosen People"* and being a part of a royal priesthood. I kept receiving guidance telling me that I had an obligation to minister and spread the Truth, but I recoiled from this. I had never wanted to minister. The idea of a life of purity and sacrifice did not appeal to a rebellious person sold on the "My Way" mentality. Plus, my speaking skills are horrible and I did not want to be exposed to ridicule and argue constantly with atheists about my beliefs and reality. The only problem was, I had already begun to minister God's Word with my online friends through sharing my experiences and debating religion.

Whether I liked it or not, my "ministry" had already begun. It was only that my ministry was a written one as opposed to spoken, and on April 12, 2009, Easter morning, the Lord guided me to Isaiah 57:18 and through visions, He directed me to write a sermon based on His Word there. I had only intended to do my usual morning activities that day and go to Easter service later, but instead, I was redirected and the rest of my morning was taken up by writing my first real sermon, which I copy here as I gave it to my online friends.

He directed me to Isaiah 57:18 today in the section titled "Comfort for the Contrite" and calls me to write to all. Call this a sermon or service if you want, but it isn't quite since I am speaking to nonbelievers as well.

Like it is said in Isaiah 57:14, *"Build up, build up, prepare the road! Remove the obstacles out of the way of my people."* And that is what I will do — for all these months He has been preparing me to be a disciple, and it is my job to cast that Light given to me onto you.

It used to be that I had no idea what Easter Sunday was all about, but I'm a quick learner and this year I know its true significance. It's not about Easter bunnies, painted eggs and candy. Those are mere distractions, for on this day you should concentrate on what Jesus did and what it means to you.

In simple terms, this is the day, the 3rd day after Jesus' crucifixion and death that he was resurrected and risen in spirit. But what does that really mean? Just a guy, some two thousand years ago who died and rose again by God's power? It is so much more than that, my friends.

God sent his Son to us as a sacrifice, the most high of sin offerings, ON OUR BEHALF because he knew our fallen nature was certain to bring us destruction. For thousands of years He saw us fail, time and time again, even his most trusted and chosen ones – the Israelites, priests and devoted servants. All of them and each one of us has committed sins – in mind, in speech and in action. Unholy we are by nature and though that is detestable in the Lord's eyes, He still offers mercy out of love.

For like in Isaiah 57:16, He says, *"I will not accuse forever, nor will I always be angry, for then the spirit of man would grow faint before me – the breath of man that I have created."*

"I was enraged by his sinful greed; I punished him, and hid my face in anger, yet he kept on in his willful ways. I have seen his ways, but I will heal him; I will guide him and restore comfort to him, creating praise on the lips of the mourners in Israel."

Israel in today's context is us, my friends – you and me and all our brothers and sisters, mothers and fathers – and the healing He promises us is through His Son, our Lord Jesus Christ. For that is why Jesus died and rose again. It was an act of sacrifice and rebirth, both literal and symbolic to make absolutely clear His message to us – that we too must sacrifice and be reborn.

Jesus' sacrifice and resurrection was also an anointment, for on that day He became the gateway by which we all must look and walk to in order to gain access to Heaven and eternal fellowship with God.

Now, I *"shout it aloud, do not hold back,"* (Isaiah 58:1) and raise my voice like a trumpet. You, me, all of us, have rebelled against God but it is also certain that He grants us healing and mercy – Grace – through our Lord Jesus Christ. By faith and belief in Him, by following his examples of sinless life, by speaking directly to Him and allowing Him to guide us. That is how we must sacrifice and be reborn in spirit.

This is not easy, I know. Yes, don't I know. I grew up on the American values of independence, think for yourself and please yourself – life, liberty and the pursuit of happiness. Our founding fathers spoke those words in context – that we have the right, the God given right, to be free and happy, but we, our generation, has taken it out of context, strayed and taken it to the far extremes of selfishness. Unfortunately, much of the world has also fallen to this mentality.

The first step to our promised healing is realizing the folly of this attitude and step out of the pursuit of self gratification and step into the right light. That step allows the next step, which is to simply acknowledge Him, our Lord Jesus, and honor his place in our lives.

That acknowledgment and honor to Him is our main goal for today, so I will leave you with that and perhaps you will catch a ray of that Light which has lit my path and as in Isaiah 58:8, *"Then your light will break forth like the dawn, and your healing will quickly appear; then your righteousness will go before you, and the glory of the Lord will be your rear guard. Then you will call, and the Lord will answer; you will cry for help, and he will say: Here I am."*

Praise the Lord, God Bless You and Happy Easter!

Bill Wilson was right. It had been a truly amazing journey – a transformation no less miraculous than a caterpillar into butterfly or coal into diamond – but my testimony here is not quite done. On May 26, 2009 the managers at my workplace called me into a meeting. It was discouraging news as it had to do with my future at the company – the place I had worked for over 15 years since I had been in college.

The economy was in and still is in a recession, and like many businesses, my company was reviewing jobs and looking for areas to cut expenses. I was told that I needed to improve my performance and do more work for the same pay or opt out with a severance package and resign.

I was crushed because even though I would have liked to get away from my job, which had grown tiresome because of the direction they wanted me to go in my work, I felt trapped. I had not graduated college and without a degree my prospects were dismal for getting a comparable paying job in a market flooded with unemployment and younger workers who did have that piece of paper and would be willing to work for much less than me.

My finances were also saturated with tens of thousands of dollars in personal debt and a mortgage. I simply could not afford to take any pay cuts. My entire paycheck went to paying the mortgage and other loans.

I felt like I was forced to stay in that job and sweat it out, but I asked the Lord for guidance and was directed to Psalm 105, which speaks of deliverance for His chosen and oppressed people by removing them from bondage, and my corresponding visions: one of a young man climbing a large, rocky hill, standing on top and then jumping into a deep valley, and the other of a farmer with a pitchfork (a symbol of self-sufficiency) all suggested that I take the other direction and resign my job.

When I had asked the Lord what am I to do instead of my regular job, I was shown a book, a hand with pen writing, a candle, and other images, which told me to write a book to share the Light and my visions. I also saw a speeding race bike, telling me to pursue motorcycle road racing and also many people standing and clapping, which I did not understand.

The book and racing I had already been told to pursue during the last few months of my guidance, and I did take steps in those directions, but it was difficult to devote the time and resources in my busy life. At this time, I only had part of the first chapter of this book written during my spare time over the period of about two months. Now the Lord was telling me to devote my full time to it.

Writing and racing... they were to be my primary missions, but I was apprehensive. I needed a steady income to pay my large bills. If I couldn't make the bills, bankruptcy and losing my home was a very real possibility. The severance for resigning would be just enough for about three months and after that I had no idea what kind of income I could get with writing and racing.

I had never written a book before and wondered, would I make enough money to get by? And racing, I had never done either and the level where I was starting had no hope for an income. I had to first prove myself on the track before I could even consider going professional. It was all too scary to consider. What if my writing wasn't good enough and what if I crash and burn on the race track?

Fear started to take hold of my conscious. I knew I was capable as a rider and writer, but good enough to do them professionally? I was not so sure about that. The race track intimidated me and just setting foot on it made me pale. I had seen the results of crashes during races – broken bones, blood, gore, and death. This was not like street riding where certainly an accident can happen at any time, but racing is putting yourself in harm's way on purpose at speeds double, triple, quadruple that of the street.

And writing too, I felt untested in. I had never published anything in my life, much less a book. Most of my writing was academic during the school years. Since then I had only written one or two short stories recounting riding adventures or other inconsequential things.

The loftiness of these goals and the uncertainty of their outcomes made me stiffen and freeze up. It was exactly like looking down into that deep valley I saw in my vision and not being able to see the bottom. In real life, unlike the vision, I was too afraid to jump, so I pondered just giving in to the demands of my job and staying with it.

Later in the evening, though, as I was preparing dinner, I heard a loud applause from the television in the next room. I usually don't have the TV on, but tonight I felt I wanted some background noise. The applause immediately triggered the vision I had earlier in the day about the people clapping, so I went quickly to the living room to see what it was. It turned out to be the end of an episode of the Star Trek Enterprise television series and showed a room full of people standing in applause just like I saw in my vision.

I thought about the show's tag line, "To boldly go where no one had gone before," and wondered if this was the reassurance I needed from the Lord to make that jump. I also remembered a piece of Scripture I was led to the week before saying, *"the righteous are as bold as a lion,"* Proverbs 28:1 and put these things together. I knew better with all the guidance I had gotten during the last six months that this was not a case of funny coincidence or wishful thinking on my part. It was a message for me to be strong and boldly continue on the path God wanted me to follow.

At that moment, I decided I would resign my job during a recession when everyone else would rather hunker down and do anything to keep their jobs. My income would be uncertain, but I had faith that the Lord was backing me up on this path, and he would provide for anything I needed.

My last day at work was June 15, 2009 and my Bible guidance in the morning as I prayed for strength and resilience in the next chapter of my life was Psalm 1, a passage that had come to mean a lot to me for many reasons, but today it was the message that the Lord watches over his believers that gave me comfort.

Blessed is the man who does not walk in the counsel of the wicked or stand in the way of sinners or sit in the seat of mockers.
But his delight is in the law of the Lord, and on his law he meditates day and night.

He is like a tree planted by streams of water, which yields its fruit in season and whose leaf does not wither.
Whatever he does prospers.

Not so the wicked! They are like chaff that the wind blows away. Therefore the wicked will not stand in the judgment, nor sinners in the assembly of the righteous.

For the Lord watches over the way of the righteous, but the way of the wicked will perish.
Psalm 1:1

That ends this chapter of my testimony – from the very beginning of my journey to the point where I am right at this moment (July 2009). Some of it is unbelievable. I know that from the standpoint of a former skeptic and scoffer.

This journey has been the most amazing set of life changing experiences that anyone could imagine. Never in a million years would I have thought I would be here, experiencing, and saying the things I am saying, but the truth is when you step forward and put full, sincere faith in Jesus Christ and follow His ways, things just start to happen. The 3rd Compass, the one that encompasses everything else – all of reality, all of wisdom, all of morality, and all of our existence – begins to spin and speak to you.

My testimony gives a sampling of how one can be guided, but everyone is not the same. Your path and guidance will be different than mine, and we will see in the next chapter how God shaped another witness with his amazing powers.

Bill Wilson's Testimony

*"If the Lord had not been on our side...
the flood would have engulfed us, the torrent would have
swept over us, the raging waters would have swept us away."*
Psalm 124:1

I introduced Bill Wilson (Skip) in Chapter One with a recounting of one of his experiences. Now I will let Skip take over in this chapter and tell his entire testimony with his own words. Here you will see that the Compass not only guides but also intervenes in our lives when we are in need.

Just A Man

This is the story of a man. Not an important man. Not a very memorable man. Just a man. My name is Skip Wilson. I was born in Tulsa, Oklahoma in 1957. These are a few of the things that have happened in my life that have led me to where I am today on this path that we call life.

This story begins in 1973. I grew up in a small town in northeastern Oklahoma. I was a member of all the sports teams we had in high school. One night we (the boys) were waiting on the girls team to get home from a game we had played in another town. We were on the edge of town in a big ditch looking across the field to my girlfriend's house about one mile away. The girls rode the bus to and from the game and were going to have a slumber party at my girl's house out in the country after the game. Us boys were going to raid their slumber party.

So we were in this deep ditch watching for the bus to turn down the driveway so we could walk across the field. There were 6 or 7 of us in the ditch when one of my buddies said, "Well, look at that," and was pointing up. We all looked up and there above us was a huge airship. It was coming in from the north at about what seemed to be 30 MPH to me. I held my arm up and laid my hand over flat and this thing showed all the way around my open hand. You could see the details on the bottom of this ship, it wasn't flat, and you could make out shadows and lights.

It went behind a cloud and turned out its running lights, then pulled away from the cloud very slowly towards the west. It was invisible if you directed your eyes at it, but if you looked at the cloud you could see it out of your peripheral vision. I told everybody how to still see it and we all did. Then the bus lights turned down the driveway and we headed for the girls where we danced and listened to music until the wee hours.

The next day I told my science teacher about it, and asked why you couldn't see it if you looked directly at it, and received a lesson on the rods and cones in your eyes. How one was for direct vision and the other was for peripheral vision. Years later, I asked the guys about the incident. One said he remembered it. Another said he didn't want to talk about it, and the rest denied it happened or said they didn't remember it.

Spun Free

This next story happened in 1974, I was 16 at the time and had an 18 year old girlfriend who lived about 40 miles away in Tulsa. We had a date and I went to pick her up only to find out she was already gone with a guy she had grown up with, who had just came back from Viet Nam. Needless to say, I was mad, so I waited on her till about midnight and then left.

I had a 1968 Dodge Coronet 440 with a six pack on it, so it would run real good. I was making my way home, still mad, when I got to a straight away, so I pushed it on down to WFO (full throttle). At this speed, my passenger wing window started to whistle from the wind, so I leaned over to shut it, so I could hear the radio better. When I leaned over I sorta pulled the steering wheel a little and eased off the road. Since I was mad, I whipped the wheel back to the right instead of easing it back onto the road. When I whipped the wheel, she started flipping.

Now my window was down and I wasn't wearing a seat belt (don't even remember if there were seat belts in it truthfully), but my spirit left my body at this point and I was floating about 30 feet to the east of the car and about 20-30 feet above it in the air. I'm facing the car as it flips down the side of the road. I can see "me" in it being slung around like a rag doll. I'm watching the car flip in real slow motion, and as it flipped down the road I moved right along with it, so I think to myself, "I must be dead because this don't happen in real life."

I figured, if I was dead I might as well get use to it and check it out, so I looked down at where my legs ought to be and couldn't see anything. I looked at my arms and could see them and my hands and the tree limbs coming right at me as I floated towards them. As I passed into and through the limbs and leaves of the trees I noticed that all my physical senses were intermingled. I could taste the green of the leaves, I could hear them. The colors made a sound and had a smell and taste.

About this time I thought, "If this is dead, it ain't so bad," so I was watching myself flip in the car and checking out my new surroundings, which I thought were pretty cool. As soon as the car stopped flipping I felt myself being drawn back into my body. The only way to describe it is like a cartoon cat being sucked into a vacuum cleaner. That's how it felt.

Next thing, I come to in the car without a scratch on me. The car is upside down in the ditch, so I crawl out through the window and climb up to the road. I hitchhiked home and went a long time without sharing this "out of body experience." Well, I did tell one person the next day, my cousin, who said I was crazy, so I didn't tell anyone else.

Held for Life

After I got out of the service back in say, 1976 timeframe, I was working offshore on the ODECO Ocean Express. ODECO's first jack up rig. I was working derricks. In the derrick you have to climb a ladder about 100 feet above the "floor" where the driller and roughnecks work. Once up there you got what we called a monkey board to stand on. You also work 12 hour days for 7 days then rotated back in for 7. So it was 7 off, 7 on.

We'd been in the Gulf and were fixing to rig her down and move locations in a few days. I'd just flew back to start my 7 day hitch on with my crew. First day back, I started up the ladder and got about 10 feet off the rig floor when I felt something touch my shoulders. It wasn't like a muscle ache, it was more like a heavy "touch" or weight. Anyways, I climbed on up the ladder and got off onto the monkey board and it went away. Did my 12 hours and came down.

Second day, I started up the ladder and got about 10 feet off the rig floor and it comes on me again, a "touch" or a heaviness on my shoulders, a little heavier this time. It stayed with me all the way up the ladder, but once I got to the top and got off on the monkey board, it went away. Did my 12 hours, came down.

Third day I start up the ladder and get about 10 feet off the drill floor and it comes on me again. This time it's on both shoulders and very heavy. It feels like I'm pushing an extra hundred pounds up the ladder with my shoulders, and I remember the previous two days and start to think, "this is weird." It starts at the same place, has gotten progressively heavier for three days now, so if I can just make it up to the monkey board, it'll be ok.

I did. Once there, it left again. I did my 12 hours and came down.

Fourth day, I started up the ladder, get about 10 feet off the drill floor and hit a wall. I AIN'T going past today. My head would go through, my arms would go through, but my shoulders hit a WALL. I backed down a couple rungs and it left. Started up with the other arm and leg first and at the same place, my shoulders hit a wall.

I crouched down and tried to push myself up through it, nope. My shoulders wouldn't go past whatever was pushing down, so I thought, ok, every day it's gotten progressively harder to climb this ladder, today I can't. Somebody is trying to tell me something, so I went back down and told the driller I didn't feel good. I asked, "Could somebody else work derricks today?" Everybody wanted my job, so somebody else started up the ladder.

The driller told me to grab a sub and rack it back on the sub rack. I was young, I was healthy, and it was only a couple hundred pounds, so I said sure.

We were working in oil based mud, which is very slick. Somehow, I slipped and slid down the v-door where we drag pipe up from the rack to the floor. Slid about 20-30 feet, no big deal except I hurt my back somewhere in the process. They called a helicopter out to the rig to take me in to the hospital.

My mom came and got me at Lake Charles hospital in Louisiana. This was my first time here as I would come back in the future. Anyways, I wake up the next morning and turn on the TV to find out my rig had sunk in the Gulf of Mexico, and later on that day they released the names and it was my whole crew that died. The guys in the other survival capsule all lived, everyone on my crew died.

Guardian angel upside down on the ladder? That's what I believe. Always have, always will.

Wax Sorrow

The next incident begins in 1979. By this time I was married and expecting our first child. I was working at a wax manufacturing plant on the graveyard shift. I remember the date, it was Friday the 13th of July, 1979. The day my first daughter was supposed to be born.

The guy I was working with was having marital problems and knew his wife was cheating while we were at work, so he brought whisky in his thermos to drown his troubles. We were changing from running one type of wax to running a harder wax, and my job was to go up on the tank and signal him when the tank was empty with a flashlight, so he could shut the belly valve and blow the line with air to clear it, so wax didn't set up in the line. I watched it run out the bottom and signaled him.

Since he'd been drinking whisky, he forgot to shut the belly valve. He did remember the air though and opened it up and blew molten wax out onto me. Since it was summer, I had my shirt off, so this molten wax covered me from the waist up, including my face, arms, and chest. I screamed like a little girl it hurt so bad. The ambulance took me to the burn center at Tulsa.

Every day they would take and peel skin and wax off of me till I couldn't stand the pain any longer, then they'd rub salve on me and wait till I could stand it again. After two weeks I was finally wax free. No new skin yet, but no wax either. A guy came to see me who'd been after me and my wife to go to church. I wasn't interested. I was riding Harleys and living the H-D lifestyle. Drinking hard, doing dope, smoking pot, whoring around, pretty much everything I wasn't supposed to be doing.

But this guy, who married one of my wife's childhood friends had been after us to give up our lifestyle, come to Jesus, and join them in church. Up till his visit in the hospital I wasn't interested, but when he showed up and asked if I wanted to pray, I said, "Friend, if you think it'll help, I'm all for it cause it hurts so bad all I want to do is die".

I got out of that hospital bed and kneeled down and we prayed. It seemed like a good long prayer, maybe 15 minutes. When we were done, we got up off the floor. I got back into the bed and he left.

The wife said, "Y'all were really into it wasn't you?"

I said, "How long did we pray?"

She said, "Over 2 hours".

She was now two weeks overdue and she left that night too. The next morning I woke up and watched as the skin literally grew back on my chest. I could watch it materializing where no skin had been a moment before.

The doctor came in and asked, "What'd you do?"

I said, "I prayed."

He said, "Whatever you prayed, it worked because you're healed. I've been a doctor here since this burn center opened up, and I've never seen anything like this. Could I write a paper on this?"

I told him, "I don't care. Can I go home because my baby is gonna be born today?"

He said, "Sure, you're well," so I checked out completely healed.

On the way home my wife's water broke and we went to a different hospital where she delivered our daughter.

Reconstructed

This next recounting of events happened in 1992, I believe. I was working in Lake Charles, Louisiana building cooling towers for GEA at a refinery. We had built two towers and was fixing to have the refinery sign off on them (saying they were satisfied and we were done), so my brother-in-law (my job superintendent) and myself could leave and go watch my mother graduate from college.

Anyway, I was giving the second tower a real close inspection and noticed some water diverters hadn't been caulked properly. I went down, got some caulking and climbed back up about 35 feet to caulk them. The structure of a cooling tower was made of wood. There's 4x4 posts standing up and bolted together, end to end, to make the tower as high as you want it. These 4x4's are tied together by 2x4, which run horizontally (with the tower) and longitudinally (across the tower). One on top of the other then spaced 6 feet apart height-wise throughout the tower.

Anyways, I was walking out on one of these bolted up 2x4's to reach the water diverter that needed to be caulked when I stepped on a 2x4 that had a knot almost all the way through it. From the top (the part I saw and stepped on) it looked good, unfortunately it was about like walking on a sheet of paper for support. It broke, and my safety line snapped too. I fell through the tower head first, breaking 2x4's on my way down. Luckily, I landed on my head.

They found me about 15 minutes later, they told me, after hearing the noise. I had crawled about 15 feet on the concrete basin dragging my head along the floor, leaving a trail of brain matter, head juice, and blood from the point of impact. My brother-in-law called an ambulance and I woke up 2 weeks later in the hospital.

The doctors hadn't seen the need to reset any bones as I kept dying on them. At one point they told my mother, "The next time he dies, lady, you better pray he stays dead, cause if he lives, he'll be a vegetable for the rest of his life."

I lost 60% of my brain mass according to the doctors. One shoulder blade was broken into 3 large parts, the other shoulder blade was shattered into a million pieces, like a windshield if it gets hit is what it looked like to me on the x-ray. Anyway, I broke just about every bone from the waist up including my skull, as I fell through the 2x4's breaking them on my way down.

When I woke up I didn't remember anything, who I was, what had happened, nothing, except my mom who was there by my side praying. She took me home because I came out of the coma and slowly I started remembering things and healing up. I remembered my daughters who I was raising by myself, but I still knew nothing of my own personality.

Was I a good guy? Was I a hell raiser? Did I drink? Did I smoke? Did I party? Did I have a girlfriend? I knew absolutely nothing about my past or who I was or what I was like. It was weird to say the least.

My friends came over and from the things they'd say I'd get a clue of who I had been. My mom would fill in the details as best she could. As time went by, I developed the personality I have now. From what everybody says, I think it's a vast improvement. See, before my accident I hadn't went to church since I was a kid. Rode a Harley and lived the lifestyle to the max. Made dope, sold dope, would fight or pull a gun or knife and use it without qualms or reservations. Was lost in sin and was so lost I didn't even know I was lost.

God in his mercy saved my life and gave me a new me, and I like the new me a lot better than the me I've heard stories about.

Flood Crossing

This next incident begins in about 1995. I'm now with my second wife, my two stepchildren, and our baby girl. We're riding home from Tulsa where we'd been grocery shopping and we're all in my grey 1987 Chevy 1 ton pickup truck. There had been rain for about a week before and the creeks were out of their banks and the roads were flooded. I turned off the interstate onto a two-lane road under construction, heading for the town that we pass through getting home.

I topped a small hill and stopped. There was water as far as I could see ahead. You could make out the trees along the road, but all you could see was water. I decided to be a smart alec and scare the wife a little, so I crept towards the water in the truck, letting it roll the front tires in a little. She looked at me like I was crazy, so I rolled in a little deeper.

I started to back out and realized, I couldn't. We were stuck and the only way out was forward. I thought about this for a minute while she prayed. Then I released the clutch and in we went, my wife calling on the name of Jesus for protection all the time we were in the water.

It turned out that the water was up to the top of the hood of the truck deep. We were going about 5 MPH and pushing a wave out in front of us. The water was up to the window on the sides and my baby daughter stuck her hand in it from her momma's lap while my wife LeAnn prayed.

I knew about where the road was. I could see the tops of the marker poles where the road workers were making the "grade" right, but I couldn't see anything but water ahead of us or on the sides. I just pointed the truck in the right direction and kept pushing water while the wife kept praying.

We made it through and came out on the other side. The wife got out to move a road barricade so we could continue on and some emergency workers floated up to us in a boat. They couldn't believe we came through that. Neither could I.

Every time I come home that way now, I look at that drop off and realize there is NO WAY that old carbureted truck should have made it. The intake was under water, the distributor cap was under water, the exhaust was definitely under water. The water should have pushed us downstream. I shouldn't have been able to keep it on what little road there was for that over two mile ride. We should have been about 30 ft. UNDERWATER from looking at it now.

A thousand reasons why we shouldn't have been able to make it through and only one reason we should. Because I had a believing wife who was praying and calling on the Name above all names in our time of need, and Jesus brought us through, or maybe He sent angels to do it, but I KNOW He's the only reason we didn't perish that day. Can't wait till I get to Heaven and meet him and tell him thanks for all the times he's saved my sorry self.

Most people see me and think, "Big ugly biker, dressed all in black leather, probably a bad dude." Then they see the Road Riders for Jesus patch on my back and ask me, "You know Jesus?"

My reply, "Yeah, I know him. Talked with him this morning. You want to meet Him?" It gives me the opportunity to pass out Bible tracts, cross pennies, or tickets to Heaven, and a chance to tell them my stories about how good God's been to me.

Wrapped In Testimony

Skip's life testimony is amazing in its own right and is a stark contrast to mine in that his experiences were much more physical. You may have noticed something about his first story, though, that didn't seem to fit with the theme of the others. In 1973 he witnessed a UFO with a handful of friends. It is something that struck me as odd at first, and you may also be wondering what do UFO's and aliens have to do with God? I almost left that part of his testimony out, but during the writing of this book I was given guidance to include and understand it. God made Skip a witness to it for a reason. We will explore this reason in Chapter Six after examining the Big Picture for the proper context in the next chapter.

Skip is "just a man," but as a direct witness to some of the most trying and amazing experiences anyone could imagine, God has made him a living example of how the invisible and intangible can affect the visible and tangible – him, you, and me. God has the power to change and save, literally, as well as figuratively. That is, in a spiritual sense, which turns out to be quite literal.

The spiritual part of reality is as real as the "visible" part, however, most of the time the spiritual part and God himself work in ways that are very subtle. My testimony highlighted the more subtle nature of his guidance, while Skip's testimony highlights the more tangible and physical aspects of it. In the next chapter, we will discuss the reasons for this subtlety – why God usually does not show his influence and power, but sometimes he does. We will also discuss just about everything else as we put the final frame around the Big Picture of Reality.

The Big Picture

"But you Bethlehem in the land of Judah, are by no means least among the rulers of Judah; for out of you will come a ruler who will be the shepherd of my people Israel." Matthew 2:6

*T*he passage in Matthew above speaks of the Shepherd, who will come out of a humble village called Bethlehem and guide his people, who, in today's context is everyone, just as I noted in my Easter sermon in Chapter Three. He is the Guide, the Light, the Compass in which I have framed reality, but many people still have trouble seeing and understanding this Big Picture of Reality.

It is enormous and difficult to grasp as a whole, but if you do not understand it completely, that is ok. You do not have to see the entire landscape in order to navigate it. All you need is the Compass. If you are more interested in understanding how to navigate your life map then skip to the next chapter, which will help you to follow Christ and use the tools he provides for us. These are the same tools I have used during my journey. However, if you are interested in a more complete understanding of the Big Picture then continue with this chapter.

The first chapter of this book introduced life maps and the notion that guides exist for us to get direction in our life maps. Chapter Two discussed the reality in which we exist and began to frame that blueprint of reality in the proper context so that it can be overlaid onto our life maps. We mixed in the solidifying agent of God and by the end of the testimonies in Chapters Three and Four the Big Picture of Reality should be forming before your eyes.

I have presented a mound of evidence and logical arguments for not just a god and creator, but the only true God. We now have the proper context that allows us to gain meaning and direction in our existence as well as understand the Big Picture.

Who is God?

The starting point for the Big Picture and everything in it is God, and so we must have an understanding of who He is. In Chapter Three, I mentioned that there are many gods in many religions, but the God I have been speaking of is the only true God. How can I dismiss all the others?

You saw in my testimony that I was not partial to any particular religion, so it is not in bias that I dismiss other gods or religions. It is simply in the evidence I was given that I can make that decision. It isn't just my personal "lottery ticket" that swayed me, but all the other evidence stacked with it.

It is a mountain of evidence consisting of scientific and logical validations of Bible content to countless witness testimonies to confirmations of our Lord Jesus Christ and the Truth throughout my journey. The evidence is overwhelmingly in favor of the God of Christianity. Still, what of the other gods and religions? What is their place in the Big Picture? We will get to that after we have looked more closely at who our God is.

In Chapter Two, I noted God as the Creator of everything, the Master Architect, and absolutely necessary for our existence and reality. In Chapter Three, I introduced God as a Guide and Compass by which we can navigate our life maps. Creator and Guide, though, are only two of God's character traits.

Other commonly spoken traits of God are: omniscience (all knowing), omnipotence (all powerful), omnipresent (everywhere at once), transcendence (outside material or physical existence), eternal (everlasting), omnibenevolent (morally perfect or good willed), perfect (in all aspects of logic, judgment and righteousness), immutable (unchanging), and personal (accessible).

These traits paint a picture of an unchanging and all powerful being without a physical body, but who is still accessible to anyone. It is an unusual combination of traits, which are in themselves also very unusual. They are so unusual and unrealistic in our everyday experience that people have attacked these traits persistently in an effort to refute God's existence. They give "proofs" based on philosophical logic and theoretical conjecture, which in the end are meaningless because their context for understanding God is completely wrong.

That context is science, that formless Blob of data, and Selective Reasoning. Science, I have argued is incomplete and incapable of probing spiritual things such as God, and atheists fall to Selective Reasoning because they simply do not understand God or His Creation (our reality and existence) and refuse to consider all the evidence for his existence, much of which I have laid out in the previous chapters.

Of course, this is understandable because I had once fallen to these pitfalls. To make the Big Picture clearer, I will describe God in terms that most people can understand. Think of him as the architect, engineer, painter, writer, and programmer of our reality. He is outside our reality just as the painter is outside the painting, the writer is outside the novel, and the programmer is outside the computer program.

Being outside of our reality gives God many of the properties I have listed simply because of this state of being. He is omniscient just as a writer knows completely the story he writes. He is omnipotent just as the programmer can change the parameters of his computer program. He is omnipresent because being outside the creation he is automatically "everywhere" in relation to it. Likewise, he is transcendent and eternal for the same reason. He has no specific location inside our reality because he is outside of it, and in the same way, he is eternal because he is not bound by our reality's timeline.

Our concept of time is bound inside our reality, but God existed before our reality and will continue to exist after our reality ceases to exist. This is how God can exist before and after time (our reality's timeline) and therefore be eternal, but that isn't the complete picture. God's eternal nature has to do with more than being outside our reality. We will explore this when we come to his immutable nature.

Our reality can be likened to a grand computer simulation where the programmer has set all the parameters, specified all the rules, and built all the mechanisms for everything to work as it does, including mechanisms for himself to interact with and influence us – the inhabitants of the creation. Simulation is a bad word, though, because it suggests our reality isn't real and is simplified in some way. On the contrary, it couldn't be any more real and is very complex and confusing.

Just think about how our reality works and that God has access to and knowledge of every part of it, including the lives, thoughts and desires of every individual in it. Billions of people and billions of lives on our planet alone are tracked and orchestrated. Clearly, an intelligence that can organize and interact with all of this information at once is beyond mind boggling. It is totally beyond our abilities to comprehend.

Fans of computer games, like "The Sims" or "Age of Empires," that allow the players to interact with the simulated inhabitants of the game can easily see how someone can be outside of the simulation and also in it. The programmers of those games built the mechanisms for that interaction, just as God built our reality and the mechanisms for him to interact in it.

However, I feel that comparing God's Creation to our simple simulations does not do justice to his work. It is only the parallel analogy that I want to convey because it shows best how God exists in relation to our reality. He is outside of it, as well as in it because of how he built it.

What I don't want to portray is that God is like a computer gamer who is only playing a game or interacting with simulated things. The nature of God, our reality, and our own purpose for existence precludes such silly notions, though, I am sure some comic personalities will draw up cartoons portraying God with coke bottle eyeglasses, staring at a computer screen, and punching at a keyboard, and exclaiming, "Why!? Why, do these little beings keep making fun of me!?"

Actually, I do recall seeing a cartoon like this years ago and I'm sure there are many more out there, but humor aside, there is a complexity to the Big Picture and our relationship with God that should be taken very seriously. The context of this relationship is a foundation for the picture we are drafting, and once we see how God relates to his creation, logical proofs rebuking his existence simply fall apart.

Two such proofs attack God's omnipotence by asking, one, if God can create a spherical cube or, two, could he create an object so heavy that even he could not lift it? The spherical cube is clearly an impossibility in our "normal" three dimensional world, but atheist's also want to attribute this impossible circumstance as a contradiction to God's omnipotence and therefore disprove his existence. God can't be omnipotent if he can't make a spherical cube. This logic is flawed because it assumes God is bound by the rules of our reality. He is not and can change any of the rules at any time.

Still, I find it an amusing thought experiment because for the spherical cube question God does not have to change anything. He already created the rules of physical reality to make the possibility possible. We know from Einstein's Theory of Relativity that space and time can be warped by gravitational fields. Space and time are therefore flexible and malleable, so all God needs to do to create a spherical cube is warp the space around a sphere such that it appears as a cube or vice versa. An easy task for someone who controls the parameters of reality.

What about the other question, can God create an object so heavy that he could not lift it? Atheists argue that either a yes or no answer will disprove the omnipotence trait and therefore disprove God, but like the first question it assumes God is bound in our reality, which is wrong.

Asking this question is like asking if an author could write about an object so heavy that his persona in the story could not lift it. The author would answer, of course, he could write that, but that doesn't mean he lost his omnipotence as the writer of the story – the author can still write anything he wishes.

Proofs like these clearly show the confusion between our reality and God's reality. They are separate things, so the proper context needs to be considered when looking at what is logical or impossible. Once the right context is used, we can see these so-called proofs against God fall away as nothing more than theories that don't fit the circumstance.

Now what about the other traits I mentioned: omnibenevolence, perfect, immutable, and personal? These traits are more confusing to understand, but they have to do with God's nature or personality instead of his state of being, which the other traits go with. Omnibenevolence, I will come to later as questions around it involve a more detailed discussion about why there is suffering in our reality.

The next trait – "perfect," in the sense that God possesses perfect logic, judgment and righteousness – is a part of his nature but also stems from being omniscient. He can see all ends in ways that limited beings such as ourselves cannot, and therefore has all the information to make the right decisions. God could never fall to Selective Reasoning.

It isn't just about decision making, though. God has a perfect sense of right and wrong, good and bad, justice and morality – Righteousness. These things overlap omnibenevolence, which I will discuss in greater detail later, but I note it here because other qualities of God flow from this – Truth, Good, Faithfulness, Justice, and Mercy. This means he never lies, never does wrong, is always loyal, always upholds justice, and is merciful.

Now, immutability. This simply means that God does not change his personality or anything else about himself. He is the God of Truth, Justice, and Mercy and will not change his mind and all of a sudden decide to be a deceitful and unjust tyrant. God can always be trusted, absolutely, because of his combined immutability and righteousness.

Immutability may seem unusual to us because who of us has never changed his mind or lied? Fortunately, God is not like us, for *"He who is the Glory of Israel does not lie or change his mind; for he is not a man, that he should change his mind."* 1 Samuel 15:29.

We are biological beings, limited, flawed, and easily corruptible through our desires, but God's immutable nature points to something very different and completely opposite. This attribute lends to his eternal nature, which was brought up earlier, and makes it not only a state of being (of being outside our reality and timeline) but also a part of his natural make-up – that of being truly immortal.

What this means to us is that God won't all of a sudden disappear like that computer gamer, who will age, deteriorate and could very well die of a heart attack after days on end of exhilarating game play, energy drinks, and pizza.

Lastly, God is personal. He interacts with us on a personal level and answers prayers. The testimonies in the last two chapters should have made that clear. Something else you may have noticed throughout the testimonies and this book is that God, Jesus Christ and his Spirit (or Holy Spirit) are used interchangeably with one another. The Bible also does this because they all function as one and are in essence extensions of the same person. They are united in relation to each other, always working in unison and always agreeing (another aspect of His immutability), as opposed to God and Satan who are opposites and separate persons.

This concept of the unity of the three holy persons is called the Holy Trinity. Some denominations of Christianity do not accept the Holy Trinity and treat God (the Father), Jesus Christ (the Son) and the Holy Spirit (or Holy Ghost) as separate. This likely came about because the concept of the Trinity is very confusing and completely different from our dealings with people in our reality.

We think of a person as a single entity, but God is different. He is outside our reality, but he also created extensions of himself in our reality so that he could interact with us. God the Father can be thought of as the part of him outside our reality, while God the Son and the Holy Spirit are the parts of him inside our reality. They are all one and the same person. Hopefully, this concept will become more clear as we continue along in painting the Big Picture.

It is no mistake, then, that the passage in Matthew quoted at the beginning of this chapter refers to Jesus as a ruler, and in Revelation he is described as the King of kings and Lord of lords. Jesus, the Son, is God and has the same authority as God, the Father.

"On his robe and on his thigh he has this name written: KING OF KINGS AND LORD OF LORDS." Revelation 19:16.

God is the supreme authority of all things and in total control, yet he is still accessible to all of us on a personal level. It sounds counterintuitive. After all, how many of us actually get to speak to a president or monarch of a country and have them listen wholeheartedly? Very few people have the ear of an earthly king, but every single one of us can have the ear of God.

How can this be? It is through his extensions of Jesus Christ and the Holy Spirit, which He provided for us to connect with him, as well as him with us. The crucifixion and resurrection of Jesus appointed a more human personality for God so that we could understand and relate to him better, while the Holy Spirit came with the appointment of Jesus so that it could act as an emissary or agent by which God can communicate with us on a continual basis.

You can think of the Holy Spirit as the Spirit of God living and acting with and inside us. This combination of Christ and the Holy Spirit, which are extensions of God himself, is the mechanism he provided for us to attain and maintain a relationship with him. I will talk more about that relationship in the next chapter.

The Composition of God

When we talk about God, the question inevitably comes up about where and how he came to be. If God created our reality and all life in it then who created him or how did he come to exist? Is there a creator for the Creator? Atheists often bring up this problem as another "proof" that God cannot exist, but the simple fact is, this conjecture is only another example of Selective Reasoning.

We do not know and do not have any means to know or verify how God came into existence because we are confined to our reality, not God's. I believe that if it were possible for us to understand God's reality, he would have already told us, just as he has told us about how our reality was created and how it relates to us.

The problem is, we are limited beings with limited capacity to understand. We can only understand reality based on the one in which we exist, so how could we understand a completely different reality? We are like the fish in an entirely water "universe." How can the fish understand what is outside their existence, such as air and land, when those things do not exist for them?

When it comes down to it, the question about where God came from does not matter at all. I can think up a hundred scenarios of how an intelligence like God could come about, but these thought experiments are fruitless when there is no way to verify God's reality other than through God himself. The logical person should move on to more important things concerning his own reality because that is what matters in his existence.

In the same way that we cannot know where God came from or how he perceives his reality, we also cannot know exactly "what" God is. Any conjecture on this would be fruitless as well without any means to verify theories, but from God's traits, what he says in the Bible, and how he interacts with us, we have some clues as to what he is.

He is certainly not like us – biological and limited – but far superior in abilities, intellect, creativity, and knowledge. Some of those abilities come from his state of being as I noted above, but where did he get all the wisdom he possesses and what is the nature of his intellect?

Again, these are areas of pure speculation on our part, but we do know that God created Man "in his image," in which he meant his spiritual and logical image, not physical (remember that God is transcendent or has no physical body). We were made to be more than the animals he created, to possess the same kind of reason and righteousness as him in potential.

God is also immutable or unchanging and eternal, so these factors suggest that God's intelligence and nature come from things that do not change or deteriorate. The only concept in our reality that may compare is energy.

Science has told us energy, such as radio waves and light, does not deteriorate unless something else interacts with it. A beam of light will continue traveling forever in the vacuum of space unless it hits something like a planet or other matter.

I make the comparison to energy not just for its unchanging quality, but also when people speak about encounters with Christ "beings" or angels they often speak of feeling an energy, like an electric pulsating sensation during the encounter. People also feel this energy during prayer, which may be the felt sensation of the Holy Spirit or God working within us and with our own spirits.

Still, when we talk about what we perceive, we are speaking in terms of our reality and not God's. God's embodiment or "presence" in our reality may be akin to a form of energy, but outside of that we can only guess based on his attributes.

Another attribute God possesses is perfect logic and reason. He is also the only god. When we put all these factors together it seems that God is the only unchanging, intelligent, and sentient (self-aware) being who exists in the true universe (the reality that God exists in, not ours). He also has the ability to reason and think through problems (cause and effect) to every level possible.

The best way I can imagine such an existence as God's is that the true universe (God's reality) is God himself – a type of neural network that formed in that reality and became God. Let me explain. Unlike our very structured reality based on superstrings, atoms and laws, a neural network (a system that processes information in a logical way) can form and function from very simple components without the need for an intelligent designer.

The computer science field of artificial intelligence gives us clues to how a neural network can form and build itself into an intelligence that can think on its own. It is completely possible that God came to exist in this way, and once his neural network was formed it cannot be destroyed or changed because there are no forces in God's reality that work against it.

Then the question of how God attained all his knowledge can be answered in the following way. His reasoning abilities are so vast that he can think through every possible combination of a problem solely with the use of his mind. We use a similar process called thought experiments in which we perform experiments in our minds using only logic. Albert Einstein is famous for coming to his revelations about space and time using thought experiments.

A being with God's reasoning abilities does not need to learn anything. He can simply "see" or follow the chains of logic to every possible outcome of every problem. Therefore, God's wisdom is not like ours. We attain wisdom by experience and knowledge but God simply "knows" because of his far superior reasoning abilities.

However, all this talk of neural networks and God's reality is only a thought experiment on my part. There is no way for us to validate God's reality, so it is best to not spin around in endless circles of conjecture and move on to topics that have more importance to us.

The Science of Creation

"God saw all that he had made, and it was very good. And there was evening, and there was morning – the sixth day. Thus the heavens and the earth were completed in all their vast array." Genesis 1:31

One thing that atheists often bring up as proof against God and Creation is the timeline of the universe and our existence being in conflict with what is stated in the Bible. Genesis chapter one clearly states that the whole of our reality, including us as humans, was made in six days. This is at odds with what science has told us, which is that the universe is over 13 billion years old, our planet is over 4 billion years old, and the life on it is nearly as old but has progressed from bacterium to complex forms, such as us, over those few billion years.

What is the problem with this discrepancy? Opponents of Creationism say that God and the Bible are wrong and therefore there is no God and the Bible is invalid, but yet again we have another example of Selective Reasoning. The context for understanding must be understood because our God is a god of truth and when he says something is true, you can bet that it is.

There is the word "context" again. I have brought it up many times now and will note why it is important to take appropriate context into account when reading and understanding God and the Bible. Some people read the Bible absolutely literally and do not take the context into account, but proper context is critical to understanding God's Word and our reality.

It is an issue of understanding the "Spirit of the Word" as opposed to the "Letter of the Word." The Letter of the Word is to take things literally. In the case of Genesis, it means that our universe and everything in it was created and formed inside our reality's timeline within six days or 144 hours, period, but science says that is impossible. This is the wrong way to interpret Genesis.

The Spirit of the Word is to take the proper context into consideration, and when we do this it becomes obvious that God is not mistaken about the six days. Think of the simulation analogy again.

It is entirely possible for someone to create a "universe" in a computer simulation within a matter of days, but inside that universe the timeline for the inhabitants is completely separate and different. Since we are confined to our reality we can only perceive what our reality tells us, which appears to be billions of years, but for God it was only a handful of days that passed in creating the universe.

God can speed up or slow down any part of our reality like we can fast forward through a video. He has complete control over all the laws of our reality, including space and time. Those billions of years that science says is needed to coalesce the universe into what we see now actually happened in the relative blink of an eye.

Genesis makes it sound like it was no difficult task at all for God to have created everything in a matter of days. After all, God simply says something and it happens, but that doesn't mean great thought was not involved in the creation. When you look closely at our reality, it is obvious that it was devised with great care, but we cannot see the entire process of the logic and decision making from our perspective. It is akin to the programmer of a simulation changing the parameters of the simulation.

The programmer (God) is aware of all the thought and processes involved in making the changes, but for the individuals inside the simulation the entire process of how the change came is hidden. The change simply becomes a part of their reality and is seemingly instantaneous. Still, the fact that God says he created all of our reality in six days gives another clue as to how vast and impressive his intelligence is.

Directed Existence

When we talk about Genesis, we talk about life, and when we talk about life, we talk about evolution or more specifically, Darwinian Evolution. The battle between Evolution and Creationism has been raging since Charles Darwin wrote "On the Origin of Species" in 1859. He brought up the notion of natural selection and postulated that all the great variety of life on earth, including humans, came about because life evolved from earlier and simpler forms by being "selected" through survival of their genes in the environment.

To put it simply, if an animal or plant is better suited for the environment then it will survive, and as it passes its genes on from one generation to the next, the traits it has that aid survival are reinforced or augmented. Over time, the augmented traits create new species, such as the giraffe evolving from a hoofed animal with a much shorter neck or whales, which are aquatic mammals, evolving from wolf-like animals that liked to hunt in the sea.

The fossil record supports Darwin's notion of evolution with countless animal skeletons that show slow progression from earlier forms to later forms over millions of years or faster. This is how science postulates that birds are descended from predatory dinosaurs, that whales and dolphins descended from wolf-like creatures, and primates (lemurs, monkeys and apes) descended from tree dwelling shrews.

What about humans from primates? For this too, there seems to be fossil evidence, so-called "missing links," which show a sequence of small lemurs progressing to monkeys and apes and finally to creatures that more closely resemble modern humans – small apes that could walk upright, such as "Lucy" the small australopithecine no larger than a modern chimpanzee and then larger forms of "ape men" like homo habilis and homo erectus. The fossil record shows these earlier forms of humanlike primates appearing through time in a logical sequence from over 3 million years ago to approximately one quarter to half a million years for our modern species of human, homo sapiens.

The fossil record is not the only evidence for evolution as DNA also reinforces the notion through shared genes. Humankind's closest living relative is the chimpanzee because more than 98% of our DNA is the same as that of a chimpanzee. The DNA of other animals can also be compared and a similar sharing and "evolution" of genes can be seen throughout the animal and plant world.

DNA and fossil evidence are very compelling proof for Evolution, but recall in Chapter Two we discussed the need for intelligent design in the workings of DNA and physical reality. It was not until we looked closer at the mechanisms for life (DNA) and reality (superstrings) that we could see a random or undirected approach could not explain these structures. Our debate on Evolution will also have to dig deeper to resolve its conflicts with Creationism.

DNA does work to create great variety in an undirected way because attributes, like hair and skin color, height, and even disposition (character traits like passivity and fierceness), can be mixed and changed through breeding alone (natural selection). However, I like to think God designed DNA to accommodate these subtle changes from the mixing of genes to show how wisdom can overpower strength, not as a means of "evolution."

That is, God did not need to go to every single plant and creature in existence and mold each one individually – one at a time – an approach often called the "brute force" method. Instead, I believe he created DNA and the mechanisms of life to produce variety of its own accord. But this is not the entire picture. He didn't just create DNA and then sit back and let it work by chance, random variance, or natural selection as most evolutionists imagine.

God also directs and orchestrates the life he created. We do not know if he molded every single living thing individually, but we do know he molded them by type or kind, such as the plants into the different kinds and animals into their different kinds. "Kinds" can be thought of as different species as well as different classes of organism, such as reptiles and mammals or bacterium and algae.

Once he created the different kinds as he saw fit, he could then sit back and watch them change into an even greater variety through the mechanisms of DNA he invented.

Then God said, 'Let the land produce vegetation: seed-bearing plants and trees on the land that bear fruit with seed in it, according to their various kinds.' And it was so. The land produced vegetation: plants bearing seed according to their kinds and trees bearing fruit with seed in it according to their kinds. Genesis 1:11

And God said, 'Let the water teem with living creatures, and let birds fly above the earth across the expanse of the sky.' So God created the great creatures of the sea and every living and moving thing with which the water teems, according to their kinds, and every winged bird according to its kind. Genesis 1:20

And God said, 'Let the land produce living creatures according to their kinds: livestock, creatures that move along the ground, and wild animals, each according to its kind.' And it was so. God made the wild animals according to their kinds, the livestock according to their kinds, and all the creatures that move along the ground according to their kinds. And God saw that it was good. Genesis 1:24

This is the essence of Creationism. It took an intelligent designer to create all the types of life we see. It is not the undirected existence evolutionists and scientists postulate. But how can we be sure of that?

Remember the inadequacy of random variance to provide structure for DNA based life and the laws of physics? It is also inadequate to create all the different "kinds" of plant and animal in existence. Without intelligent direction, an amoeba is not going to a become a shellfish or a shellfish into a fish or fish into an amphibian and so on down the chain until we get to us as humans.

Evolutionists suggest that only random variance and the selection of traits for the changing environment is sufficient to create all the kinds of life we see. The problem is that I have already shown that random cannot provide structure or direction of any kind, and natural selection can only go so far in producing changes in an organism. Changing skin color is a far different problem than creating new kinds of limbs and other more complicated structures that differentiate between the species.

Look at it more closely to see the problem with Evolution. We have to go right down to the DNA code. If you start making random changes to it, the structure falls apart and the code fails to produce a viable life form, just as a story loses comprehension if words are randomly changed or added to it. Geneticists already know this aspect of DNA – that it is very structured and simply changing things at random is fruitless.

To properly direct useful changes into the code of DNA or any code for that matter, such as the words of a story, intelligent changes or additions need to be made in the correct places and in the correct sequence. Without this kind of intelligent direction, a life form as complex as us would be impossible if it started out as bacterium.

In the case of life then, it was God that made these modifications, not the environment, natural selection, and randomness. If evolutionists were completely right, then biologists could just zap bacterium in a dish with radiation or simply insert or move around the chemical strands to randomly change the DNA and all kinds of different life forms would spring out of that dish. Instead, all they accomplish is to kill the bacterium because random changes only work to make the code of DNA fail.

Randomness cannot direct the changes needed to evolve one kind of life into another, but God did create DNA to allow for a large amount of variety on its own. There is a limit, though, to the amount of change that can come from natural selection alone.

It can produce great variety. For instance look at the class of arthropods called insects, which have six legs and a three part body plan – head, thorax, and abdomen. It is the largest and most varied animal group on our planet consisting of millions of distinct species, but all of them conform to the same body plan and most have not changed by any significant amount over hundreds of millions of years.

The lowly ant was here over a hundred million years ago, appearing just as it does today. Where is the great diversification into different life forms over those millions of years that Darwinian Evolution promises? That is more than enough time for the environment to change and for natural selection and random variance to work its wonders, right? But there are no grand changes for the ant and insect kingdom because when left undirected, natural selection only creates variations upon the same theme.

There are big ants, little ants, red ants, black ants, ants that march in an armed mass to gather food, and ants that farm fungus for food, but they are all still ants. The same stagnation of evolution can be seen in many other parts of the plant and animal kingdom. Natural selection can only provide great variety once certain plans or kinds have been created.

The biologist, though, will bring up the stages of life from single-celled organisms like bacteria and protozoa, to more complex forms of aquatic life like crustaceans, to hard shelled, "armored" fish, to scaled fish, to air breathing soft skinned fish, to amphibians, to reptiles, to mammals, and onward to humans. The sequence appears logical, doesn't it?

But ask yourself where all the extra DNA code came from that is needed to build these more complex organisms? Bacteria and viruses only have a genome (the entire genetic make-up or length of the DNA code) in the tens of thousands while more complex organisms have billions. We know that random additions to code don't work and natural selection only makes more subtle changes. It cannot add or modify code in the ways needed to build new types of life.

And to further the confusion, the animal with the largest known genome is also one of the smallest and simplest. Certain classes of amoeba have a huge genome of hundreds of billions while humans have less than three billion. Why is that? Are segments of code simply redundant and useless? Some biologists think so, but no one knows for certain because we don't have the knowledge to fully interpret the DNA code.

Also consider the appearance of flowers and their pollinators (bees, butterflies, birds, bats, etc.) in this debate. Evolutionists know that flowers appear in the fossil record very suddenly about 130 million years ago. It was as if they just magically appeared out of nowhere. Charles Darwin himself was confused by this and stated that their evolution was "an abominable mystery." That mystery remains today over a century and a half later.

Flowers are complicated structures for the reproduction of

their parent plants. They include male and female components that act just like the corresponding parts in the animal world. They also include components like petals and scent glands that are designed to attract their pollinators. How can such a complex design that is tailored so well for the symbiotic relationship between plant and animal just appear suddenly without any previous models that lead up to it – so-called missing links?

The most common pollinators, insects, had been around for hundreds of millions of years before the first flower appeared. You would think that there would be evidence of a symbiotic relationship or "coevolution" of plant and animal over those hundreds of millions of years that shows gradual changes in the plants that develop into those flowers, yet the fossil record shows no evidence for it. Flowers simply bloom out of a vacuum of existence.

To explain this, let's look at the DNA code once again. Biologists have sequenced the DNA of many flowering plants and found that like in the animal kingdom, there are genes that when turned on and off are responsible for producing different structures, such as developing a leg as opposed to an antenna in insects or a petal and other floral structure instead of a leaf for plants. How are these genes significant in this debate?

Their very existence is the key. Recall the structure of DNA, that it is like an instruction book laid out by sequence (sentence), gene (paragraph), and chromosome (chapter). It is a code where the order and interaction between different sections is important, and furthermore, the code must be complete and structured for it to be useful. Randomness is not a viable means for changing or introducing code as we have already discussed.

These genes in both animals and plants are complete in that they define how entire structures are built, not parts of it, like a piece of a leg or vein of a petal, but the **entire** structure. How can the complete code of the whole structure (the gene) be created without intelligent direction and design? Assuming genes came about randomly is like assuming entire paragraphs where inserted into a book, complete and coherent, by random chance alone.

If it was only random changes and natural selection that created these genes then there should be much more DNA code for everything as more and more code is added to the instruction book and randomly mixed about. Organisms as complicated as ourselves should have a million times more code than that amoeba, but that isn't the case.

Somehow, the appropriate DNA code was inserted into the instruction book and unnecessary code was taken out. A random or unintelligent process like Darwinian Evolution and natural selection is completely incapable of such intelligent maintenance of the DNA code. However, God's intelligently directed Creationism is. Confusing?

It certainly is. This aspect of reality was designed to confound us, so distinguishing between which forms of life were molded directly by God and which came about from breeding alone may be an impossible task. There is really only one organism on our planet that we are assured of knowing was designed directly by God, and that is us, humans.

If God directed how life was created, then why does the fossil record and evolution appear to show a logical progression from bacterium to aquatic life to land based life in small increments and steps over eons, including increments from primates to man? God could have created only man and the life forms that we need for food. Why create everything else like all the animals that are now extinct and the ones that are a nuisance? I, for one, could definitely live without mosquitoes.

This is the confusing part of reality I alluded to earlier and the reason for it is another aspect of the Big Picture. It is the same reason why the timelines for the universe and planetary processes were made to appear in contradiction to statements in the Bible, the reason for the enormous vastness and variety of our visible universe and the life forms on earth, and the reason why our entire reality was constructed with so many layers – the seen, tangible and scientifically testable, physical layers and the unseen "spiritual" layers. Our reality was constructed in a confusing and confounding way, and that is no accident. This leads us to our next section which brings us back to that trait of God I skipped earlier, omnibenevolence.

Reason for Suffering

Omnibenevolence – In strict literal terms is defined as the quality of having infinite benevolence, where benevolence is defined as the desire to do good to others or the expression of kindness, goodwill and charity. In theological context, omnibenevolence further extends the notion of "good" and is taken to mean God is infinitely or perfectly good, just and moral. God's mercifulness, faithfulness, and righteousness stem from this quality and so completes the list of traits that deal with his morality.

Omnibenevolence is a quality of God that is very hard to understand in the reality that many of us perceive today – one that is full of rage, hate, violence, and moral atrocity. How can a God that is omnibenevolent create a reality that would allow such horrible things to happen? Not a day passes today without news of a murder, an abused child, hate crime, sex crime, or some other form of moral injustice. It is enough to make someone ignore the news entirely, and indeed, people do just that.

Aren't we all tired of it – being saturated in the heavy fog of repugnant crimes? No matter what we do to run away, brush it off, or wave it away, it lingers and clings to us with a persistence that breeds fear. We buy guns, tasers, alarms, and pepper spray to defend ourselves. We take self-defense classes, change our behavior, and teach our children to be better prepared so that we may not be victims.

The reality of this fog is another confounding example of a very complex and bewildering Creation – an existence created by an omnibenevolent God that appears to be in contradiction of that very trait. It is a contradiction that atheists have jumped on persistently in an effort to crush the notion of God entirely.

They often bring up Bible passages that show God's seeming lack of benevolence, such as the many instances of God enacting punishment on individuals and nations alike, bringing plagues, issuing commands to kill and slaughter, and so on. God even symbolizes his wrath with *The Cup of God's Wrath.*

Take from my hand this cup filled with the wine of my wrath and make all the nations to whom I send you drink it. When they drink it, they will stagger and go mad because of the sword I will send among them. Jeremiah 25:15

Atheists say, "Look, God is malevolent, not benevolent!" and so cannot be omnibenevolent and therefore cannot exist. Once again, though, this line of thought is too simple and suffers from Selective Reasoning because the entire context, the Big Picture, needs to be considered.

Let us first look at the notion of "good." By all definitions which are not nouns or things, "good," is a state in relation to another state. Good cannot exist on its own, but must be qualified on a scale or compared to another state. Without comparison, we cannot know that something is good or not. How can we judge if a car is good to purchase if we are not comparing it to some standard?

Morality, another aspect of "good," works in the same way. Someone who is morally good is being judged or compared to some standard in order for them to be labeled good, so it is impossible for good to exist without the opposing qualifier, which is not good – bad – or in the context of morality, immoral, unjust or even evil.

A reality in which good exists, then, cannot be made without bad. Both concepts necessitate one another and a reality without one or the other would be a reality in which there is no choice of one direction or another, one decision over another, or one state over another.

From an engineering standpoint, all the logic flow charts in that reality would be a simple straight line from problem to solution. There would be no branching in logic from selecting Choice A, Choice B, or Choice C. Zero decisions can be made in such a "single-state reality" because there is only one choice or single direction to go.

Any beings in such a reality would only be automatons set to go in one direction, mere wind up toys that do the same thing over and over again, so anyone who argues that a "perfectly good" God should have also created a "perfectly good" reality, where only good can happen, does not have a complete understanding of the concept.

They are suggesting that God create a reality in which there is no choice – no free will. That kind of reality would be as interesting as watching a clock tick. No matter how ornate or intricate one makes the mechanisms of the clock, all it does in the end is tick away the time in an all too predictable way.

Fortunately, God is interested in far more than watching clocks tick. He created our reality and us so that we could have free will – the ability to choose any direction we wish. The main reason for this I am building up to, but at the moment we are talking about benevolence. Our reality, then, with all its choices and possibilities cannot exist without good and bad together.

Good and bad existing together does not mean God needs bad or cannot exist without it. This would be confusing our reality with God's reality. Remember that they are separate, and God's intellect is wholly apart from our reality.

Many theists say that God *is* good or embodies it. This is true because God defines good and he stands for what is good. He is righteous. God also defines what is bad, though, but that is not the same as saying that God is bad or evil. He defines all of our morality and universal notions of good and bad. It was done our sake, so we could have a reality with free will and be able to discern good and bad.

I think everyone can concede that concepts of good and bad are needed to define each other, but does a god who punishes and shows wrath, as ours clearly does, contradict omnibenevolence? To answer that, we need to move further into the notion of "good," into the realms of morality.

Omnibenevolence also means that God has a perfect sense of morality and justice – perfect righteousness. Earlier in this chapter, I mentioned that this trait also comes from being omniscient. God knows all things and therefore has the foresight to make absolutely good judgments. He can see the consequences of actions which in turn trigger further actions and consequences that we as limited beings cannot fathom as a whole.

Our judgments rely on our limited perspectives and knowledge, but God is fully informed of every aspect of our reality. He can make the decisions that will prove most beneficial to the overall good, which brings us full circle back to the literal meaning of benevolence – the

desire to do good or express goodwill to others. God and our reality do not contradict omnibenevolence because he does **desire** good to be had, but in a reality that consists of good, bad, and everything in between, a balance needs to be made that tips in the favor of the **overall good**, which may contain some very bad things, such as the suffering from disease or one person needing to die so that many more will benefit.

We are limited beings with limited perspectives in our reality and must acknowledge that to understand how God is omnibenevolent in a reality filled with hardship, suffering, and punishment. An omniscient God can determine without fault who should be disciplined and by what means.

The punishment can be as forceful as death, which may seem like a barbaric thing to an "evolved" society, but the truth is, we are still as limited in perspective as we were thousands of years ago – constantly and consistently falling to Selective Reasoning.

Whenever the Bible speaks of God's wrath or anger, it is actually a righteous anger caused by wrongdoing and not the same anger as the Sin of Wrath, one of the Seven Deadly Sins, that we have been told not to fall to. The difference is important because anger and punishment that are justified should not be confused with that which is not.

A good example of how limited our perspective is can be seen with the disputes of capital punishment in our judicial systems. Do we have the right to condemn people to death? That discussion could take an entire book to engage in, but when it boils down to the absolute, the fact remains that we as individuals, as groups, as nations, and as societies are capable of making mistakes because of our limited way of seeing the world.

That is why God has told us not to judge.

"Do not judge, or you too will be judged. For in the same way you judge others, you will be judged, and with the measure you use, it will be measured to you." Matthew 7:1.

We can **and have** condemned innocent people to death, so who are we to make judgments on God's judgment? If we say that God's punishments are too extreme or not right, we are judging God by our own flawed and limited standards, which is a clearly substandard ruler for measuring an omniscient being.

Our limited perspectives are exactly why is it not good enough to simply "be good and do no harm to others" – a popular mantra for our new age of politically correct, "enlightened" society. Who's rules are you conforming to when you do this, and how do you know for certain you are doing no harm, not just to others but yourself as well? Just as with capital punishment this issue boils down to the absolute. We do not know all ends to our decisions and how it affects the overall good and our own overall good.

The "be good" mentality is just a compact way of saying, follow our own rules, whatever WE think is right, because all of us have different experiences, predispositions, and viewpoints. It is a self-centered sense of morality that actually opposes true righteousness, which is not based on any individuals' or groups' sense of right, but on the overall good that only an omniscient and omnibenevolent God can perceive.

We try to protect our children with our own judgment because we see that they do not have the experience or wisdom to make the right decisions. They may resist, scoff, or even belittle our decisions because of their willful short-sightedness, but we still try to instruct and discipline them (in some cases forcefully), for their overall good. In relation to God, we are all just as willful children resisting the guidance of someone with much greater experience and wisdom than us.

Sometimes, though, we are too willful to take the counsel of a wiser person. How would you treat that dissenting person? If he was a minor, then we as adults could force better behavior on him, or if he was part of the military or another institution which strictly enforces behavioral standards, he could be forced to conform as well.

Most of the time, though, we do not have the authority or right to force behavior on someone. We would be called dictators if we did, and it would be unlawful and immoral to do so since we would also be removing a God given right from that person – free will. In cases where bad behavior may threaten someone's well-being, yet it is still a lawful behavior by our standards, and they have not taken advice to change, then our only choice is to let them be and have them go their own way.

God, however, has the right to enforce his moral standards at any time, and may punish with as much force as death, but most of the time, he will simply let willful people be and not try to influence them in order that free will be maintained. This may not sound like a punishment, but it actually is, because once we are left to our own devices, our Compass and guidance towards our "overall good" is gone, and we end up stumbling again and again in the darkness of our poor, short-sighted decisions, or worse, we succumb to the forces that oppose God's will and desire for benevolence.

These forces have to do with the entire fallen nature of our existence – the battle with sin or anything which opposes God's will for the overall good. This is a spiritual battle we will discuss later. My point here is that not only do we not have the foresight to choose what judgment is appropriate, but the "let them be" treatment for those who are overly willful is another reason we find great suffering in our reality. God will simply not help anyone who refuses his help, as he states in Psalm 81:11, *"But my people would not listen to me; Israel would not submit to me. So I gave them over to their stubborn hearts to follow their own devices."*

God's omniscience and omnibenevolence make him the perfect judge, but still, why the need for punishment? There are so many Biblical examples of God upholding justice by judging, rewarding and punishing that it could fill an entire book. The faithful are rewarded for their efforts and devotion to God while punishment shares an equal role in Biblical history.

Right from the very beginning in Genesis, God punishes Adam and Eve for eating from the tree of the knowledge of good and evil, which condemns the whole of humanity afterward to battle sin, corruption, and death, and later in Genesis, Noah and his family are spared mankind's first global punishment for his righteousness. Judgment, reward and punishment continue all the way up to the last chapter, Revelation, which prophecies the final punishments for mankind and the redemption of the faithful. Justice, judgment, reward and punishment appear to go hand in hand but unlike good and bad, which cannot exist without one another, these extensions of morality can. Or can they?

Morality is a sense of what is right and wrong – the rules laid down to discern right and wrong. Justice is the quality of being just or morally right. In a reality that has the potential for right and wrong acts, justice is akin to the balance scale tipping in favor of the overall good or right. Judgment is to determine whether something falls on the right or wrong side of the scale using the rules of morality, while reward and punishment are the consequences of being in the right or wrong.

Atheists argue that an omnibenevolent god should have made

a reality without the bad consequences or punishment in the case of justice. I stated earlier that good and bad must exist together, so bad cannot be completely taken out of the equation. But punishment can. What happens when we take away punishment and only have reward?

This would be a reality with only positive reinforcement in psychological terms. Since we would still be free to choose bad acts but not have the consequence of punishment, there would be nothing to deter our reasoning from committing bad acts. People would reason that, though a reward may come for a good act, a bad act will do no harm and so they might as well do it if it is desirable to them. The frequency of bad acts would then increase more than the good and the overall good or justice could not be maintained.

Taking away punishment would be the same as eliminating our law enforcement and judicial system. That would result in a society overrun by immorality. A reality like that would obviously contradict the "perfectly good" reality that atheists imagine from an omnibenevolent god.

Punishment must go with reward for justice to be upheld. Therefore, our reality was built as just or "perfectly good" as an omnibenevolent God can make while also giving us the ability of free will, which necessitates the options of both good, bad, and everything in between.

Indivisible Necessity

Good and bad, right and wrong (morality), and all the options in between are necessary for the kind of existence that God intended for us – one that gives us free will and where justice can be maintained – but those are not the only reasons God designed our reality this way. Let me call this kind of reality a Free-State Reality as opposed to the single-state, "no choice" reality I had mentioned before, so that the notion can be encompassed in a single term without having to say good, bad, right, wrong and everything in between.

God designed our Free-State Reality so that we could be less like animals and more like himself – possessing a higher kind of intelligence. One aspect of that higher intelligence is the ability to experience pleasure or joy – the satisfaction of something that is appealing or attractive to us. Appealing and attractive are more concepts that need the qualification of a standard to compare one thing with another, just like good and bad, one cannot determine if something is appealing if there is not an idea of what is unappealing. Without any rules or scale of what is good to us, pleasure could not exist.

Hope is another part of a Free-State existence. Like pleasure, it needs notions of what is better than something else. You cannot hope for a better thing or circumstance if there is no discernment for what is better. We can see now that a reality without the rules and options of a Free-State Reality is also one without free will, pleasure, hope, or justice. Goodwill and mercy would also be absent because the notion of "good" is gone.

We would be absolutely emotionless beings or at least not have true emotions as we know them. It is possible to have "emotions" in a single-state reality by having purely instinctual behavior, but they would merely be "wired" responses, such as fear triggered by a threat or lust triggered by pheromones.

God created our reality and us to be much more than ticking clocks and pre-programmed robots. He created us to be like him, with higher intelligence, emotions, free will, and morality. He created our Free-State Reality to enable these things. Our reality, with all its bad and good components, is essential for sentient, intelligent life to exist and because our God is also omnibenevolent and omniscient, he can and does see to it that events happen for the overall good, not just for humanity as a whole but for individuals as well. That is why we can trust God to be our personal Guide and Compass.

It is only in our limited perspectives that we sometimes cannot understand why things are as they are or why there is suffering and hardship. I stated earlier that we are just like children to God, naive in existence, just as our children are to us, but there is perfectly good reason for suffering, punishment, and discipline. Sometimes we do not see that, but a perfectly omniscient and omnibenevolent God does.

"My son, do not make light of the Lord's discipline, and do not lose heart when he rebukes you, because the Lord disciplines those he loves, and he punishes everyone he accepts as a son." Endure hardship as discipline; God is treating you as sons. For what son is not disciplined by his father? ...

Our fathers disciplined us for a little while as they thought best, but God disciplines us for our good, that we may share in his holiness. No discipline seems pleasant at the time, but painful. Later on, however, it produces a harvest of righteousness and peace for those who have been trained by it. Hebrews 12:4

In this discussion about good and morality, we can see now why our reality has suffering and how God fulfills omnibenevolence. He created the possibility of good and bad and set the rules of morality so that we could have a higher order of intelligence and existence – that we would know hardship, sorrow, and hopelessness in order that we could also know freedom, joy, and hope. However, there is a greater motivation for why God created reality and us as he did.

Sentience and true emotions are wonderful, but there is something more.

It is the pinnacle of emotion – the very tip of the Eiffel Tower in Paris. Poets and artists have been inspired by it for centuries, and the passage in Hebrews above alludes to it. It is Love. No other word is so short, yet so full of meaning and confusion. Those who yearn for it are emptied of their hearts, but those who have found it true, have their hearts filled forever.

God is a fully feeling and emotional being, and indeed, many theologians describe God simply as Love personified. In fact, it becomes obvious to anyone who learns and comes to know God on a personal level that love is THE basis for our existence.

God knows love, and I can think of no better way to show omnibenevolence than for him to create beings in order that they may also know love and for them to love him back, just as we desire to have children out of love and for them to return it.

Love is so important, in fact, that it is spelled out for us explicitly as The Greatest Commandment:

"Love the Lord your God with all your heart and with all your soul and with all your mind." This is the first and greatest commandment. And the second is like it: "Love your neighbor as yourself." All the Law and the Prophets hang on these two commandments. Matthew 23:37

A Solid Blueprint

The first chapters of this book laid out that our structured reality is impossible without intelligent direction. In this chapter, I discuss further the need for intelligent direction for the great variety of life and in our own existence. And now after talking about omnibenevolence, we also see that our Free-State Reality was created so that we could have higher orders of intelligence (free will, morality and emotion).

God is the originator of all order, logic, morality, and even love in our reality. The rules and logic were set for us by him, but people still relent and suspend belief of God despite the massive amount of evidence. They persist in seeing reality only with the probing sticks of science, which simply cannot provide the context to understand reality in its truest form.

Once again, this is understandable because our reality was made in a deliberately confusing way. Everything from the properties of the universe, to the apparent sufficiency of Darwinian Evolution, to the invisible nature of God and the spiritual world were designed this way.

The sheer vastness and amount of variety in the cosmos seem to support the sufficiency of random variance for our existence. The great variety and adaptation that DNA provides and the evidence in favor of Darwinian Evolution also seem to support an undirected existence. That is, on the surface.

It is only when we examine reality closer and pick apart its constructs, we find that things are very different. God and intelligent direction are required for all aspects of our reality to make complete, logical sense.

The very foundations of our reality and existence were laid down in this way to confound and test us. This is same reason why

Jesus spoke to the masses in parables or riddles using symbolism, but to his disciples he spoke plainly, as he told them, *"The secret of the kingdom of God has been given to you. But to those on the outside everything is said in parables so that, 'they may be ever seeing but never perceiving, and ever hearing but never understanding; otherwise they might turn and be forgiven!'"* Mark 4:10.

This sounds like knowledge is being withheld on purpose and seems unfair, but we must be careful not to jump to conclusions and judge God, for we are so limited in understanding. When Jesus said this, he meant that the secret to the kingdom of God is so valuable that it is akin to a great jewel or treasure and cannot simply be given away, but the recipients must be tested and filtered.

I did not pass the filter myself because science and my leaning towards "free thinking" had led me astray. I was overconfident in myself and in what simple reasoning and the Blob of Science told me. However, our reality was designed to confound those who have an excess of pride in their own viewpoints.

Pride, number one of the Seven Deadly Sins, is so insidious and gives birth to so many other sins that our entire reality was fashioned to make the prideful stumble. Even the Twelve Apostles of Jesus suffered from this, knowing that they had knowledge of the kingdom of heaven and access to Christ himself, and so they asked who among them was the greatest:

At that time the disciples came to Jesus and asked, "Who is the greatest in the kingdom of heaven?"

He called a little child and had him stand among them. And he said: "I tell you the truth, unless you change and become like little children, you will never enter the kingdom of heaven. Therefore, whoever humbles himself like this child is the greatest in the kingdom of heaven." Matthew 18:1

The seriousness of Pride is not to be taken lightly considering that so much of our true and hidden reality, the Big Picture of which I am explaining, was made to be concealed to the prideful. The conceit that pride in our own logic gives us, is, of course, a product of the Free-State Reality that God intended, but he knew this and *"By wisdom the Lord laid the earth's foundations, by understanding he set the heavens in place, by his knowledge the deeps were divided, and the clouds let drop the dew."* Proverbs 3:19.

In other words, God saw what bad things Pride would bring right from the beginning, and so devised reality to filter it and created the ultimate reward for virtues opposing it – *"Take your inheritance, the kingdom [of heaven] prepared for you since the creation of the world."* Matthew 25:34.

Humility is one of those virtues opposing Pride – *"Blessed are the meek for they will inherit the earth"* Matthew 5:5. The reward of the kingdom of heaven was made for those who could humble themselves and show respect, not just to God, but to all their fellow humans. The first and second greatest commandments in which I ended the last section reflect this thinking, *"Love the Lord"* and *"Love your neighbor,"* and further emphasizes how important this issue of controlling pride is.

Pride leads to conceit, stubbornness, selfishness, vanity, greed, deceit, blind ambition, and a frequent term in this book, Selective Reasoning. It is also a primary reason for the fall of one of God's most highly appointed angels, Satan. The angels were created with free will and higher intelligence just as mankind was, but Satan had so much pride that he thought he could trump God and replace him, and so began a war – that spiritual war, which was mentioned earlier.

The real confusing thing, though, is that God planned the war and created Satan for a reason. We touched on this need for "bad" during the discussion about omnibenevolence. Sin was molded out of the rules of morality in order for us to fully realize redemption, peace, and pleasure through suffering, hardship, and pain. Sin is commonly understood as simply "wrongdoing," but actually it is anything (any thought, speech, or action) that moves us away from God and his will – that greater overall good, which of course includes "wrongdoing" or immoral behavior.

On the side of sin, Satan was created as an adversary to God, a leader, ruler, and instigator for the opposing side in this spiritual war, and with him came one-third of God's angels, who are now called demons. Now, of course, when some people hear about angels and demons they begin to roll their eyes, but recall in Chapter One that a survey found almost 70% of the general population believes that angels and demons are active in our world today. The reason for this large majority is very simple, and it is not because the population is filled with superstitious, irrational, delusional people.

Another aspect of the Big Picture is that the Bible is absolutely correct and everything it states about the spiritual world is also true. Not only do God and Jesus Christ exist but angels and demons as well. There are multitudes of witness accounts on all of this, which cannot simply be dismissed as I pointed out at the end of Chapter Two. You may wonder, though, why haven't I heard of or experienced anything out of the ordinary?

One reason is not that the spiritual world does not exist, but that experiences with the spiritual world are so out of the ordinary and can be so intense or profound that people are afraid to discuss them out of the fear of appearing crazy or delusional.

There are other reasons why you may not have noticed spiritual things too, Selective Reasoning being one of them, but the truth is, the dark forces in this spiritual war would rather stay concealed and let you believe they do not exist because they work to influence us through the invisible mediums of emotion and thought, through Sin and temptation, and through our natural biological tendencies for self indulgence and selfish pursuits.

The spiritual world works in very subtle ways 99% of the time, not just because of the invisible, intentionally confounding nature of our reality but also because of the importance of free will. I call this the Coercion Factor, which is another reason why the spiritual world is usually hidden to us and why God does not come out in broad daylight and announce himself... most of the time.

There are instances in the Bible where God and other spiritual beings like angels appear to man but in every case where the spiritual beings do not disguise themselves as only human, the people are absolutely frightened by the encounter. *"Do not be afraid,"* is a common directive from angels, and anyone who has witnessed these beings to this day can attest that fear is often the first reaction in the encounter.

If God and spiritual beings were constantly shown to us and exhibiting their far greater powers and "unnatural" properties, our free will would be demolished because we would be coerced through fear to obey God's directives. A coerced existence is not the kind of reality God wants for us.

He wants free will for us and designed our Free-State Reality to accommodate it. He knew all the aspects of our reality and the possibilities of great evil and suffering in it. That is unavoidable with free will.

The spiritual war is an aspect of the "bad" part of this reality. It affects every single one of us whether we are aware of it or not, and it leads me to our next section about how that spiritual war and the Big Picture affects religion as a whole.

Schematic of Religion

Absolutely confounding our reality is, and for good reason, but I have only touched on the major aspects of the Big Picture. Another issue full of contention is that of one religion over others. But once the entire context of reality is understood, it is easier to see how religions relate to the Big Picture.

Easier to see, but still a complicated issue that is beyond the scope of this book. It is complicated because there is no absolute right and wrong, but varying degrees by which a particular religion conforms to the Truth of the Big Picture that Christianity gives us.

It may sound conceited to state that Christianity provides us with the best and most complete portrait of the truth of our reality, but frankly, it is a simple matter of statistics. There is no other religion that is backed up by so much real world evidence, no other that can explain with so much accuracy the nature of the spiritual realm, and no other that can explain so well what is going on with my life as well as everyone else's.

Recall our discussion about superstring theory in Chapter Two and that, like Christianity and God, it has enough evidence to be taken seriously. So much evidence, in fact, that the probability of it being true is at or near 100%. The evidence for Christianity is no different, and so it can be set as the standard by which other religions are compared.

This also means the accuracy and validity of the Bible is at or near 100% and indeed God's Word was given to us for much more than to merely record witness testimony and human history. It is a divinely inspired work given to us as a tool and standard, a ruler, to measure Truth. It is another part of the Compass that encompasses everything, and as a guide combined with the Big Picture, it can be used to evaluate the other religions of the world.

Some religions are truly as atheists charge, fully concocted by mankind as a means to understand the universe, but have little or nothing to do with the true nature of reality. Others are similar but were devised by unscrupulous people to manipulate and control people. The terms cult, brainwashing, and coercion are often used with these kinds of religions. The probability of these being able to explain reality fully is near zero.

Still other religions come closer, perhaps up to 50 percent of the Truth, because they are based on human observations of the spiritual world through centuries of effort and exposure – basically a "scientific" probing of the spiritual realm. But just as scientific probing of the natural world overlooks essential aspects of reality, spiritual probing errors in the same way. I would consider religions that rely only on concentrated meditation and the realization of your "inner self" as fitting this description. Many aboriginal and tribal religions may also fit here.

Then there are the religions that come very close to getting the whole picture but miss important aspects of it. The religion in which Christianity shares its history with, Judaism (the religion of Israel and the Jews), falls here because though the Israelites are the original chosen people of God, they do not acknowledge Jesus as the living and resurrected Christ – the prophet messiah they were instructed to wait for. This is a very important part of the Big Picture that we will examine later.

There are also religions that twist and distort the Big Picture. Islam falls here because it stems out of the roots of Christianity, but unfortunately, its nature signals a more misleading quality. It was founded over 500 years after the time of Jesus and after the latest writings of the New Testament in the Bible. It includes material from Judaism and Christianity, such as the Hebrew Torah (parts of the Christian Old Testament), the Psalms of David (also part of the Old Testament), and the Gospels of Jesus Christ (parts of the New Testament) but changes were made to their content in ways that are conspicuous.

This is the first sign of misdirection because I stated earlier that the Bible and God's Word were given to us as a ruler and standard so that we could discern reality and judge right and wrong.

One example of the twisting of original Scripture is that in Islam the child of promise from whom God's chosen people descend is Ishmael instead of Isaac. Both were begotten from Abraham (the man chosen by God to be the father of his chosen people), but Isaac came from a union with Sarah, Abraham's wife, while Ishmael came from a union with Sarah's servant, Hagar, whom Abraham took as a concubine.

Ishmael was born first, but the Bible clearly shows that the descendents of Isaac are the chosen people of God, the Israelites. The descendents of Ishmael, however, go on to found Islam through the prophet Muhammad, an interesting twist in the favor of Islam. There are many other changes and addenda to the original Scripture that appear strategically made, and in the end, Islam paints a very different picture of God and its version of truth.

Another sign of misdirection is how the Islamic holy book came to be. Consider that the contents of the Bible were penned by dozens of people across thousands of years and across cultures, yet the messages of all those writings synchronize and reinforce each other. This is because all of it was directed and inspired by the one true God.

The Qur'an or Koran, however, was penned by one man, Muhammad, supposedly by revelations from the angel Gabriel in a period of about two decades. I say "supposedly" because how did Muhammad know he was actually communicating with one of God's trusted messengers? Muhammad simply took the spiritual being's word for it and did not test the spirit as the Bible instructs us to:

Dear friends, do not believe every spirit, but test the spirits to see whether they are from God, because many false prophets have gone out into the world. This is how you can recognize the Spirit of God: Every spirit that acknowledges that Jesus Christ has come in the flesh is from God, but every spirit that does not acknowledge Jesus is not from God. 1 John 4:1

The need to test the spirits is simple. They can appear to us in many forms and the evil ones do so in ways to deceive, *"for Satan himself masquerades as an angel of light."* 2 Corinthians 11:14. In a world where a spiritual war is in place, we must be wary of the agents that oppose God, so as Apostle John says, we must test the spirits.

All spirits from God will acknowledge that Christ came *"in the flesh,"* meaning that Jesus was God incarnate (the actual Son of God) on this earth, and I can say that Muhammad did not test the spirit he was communicating with because Islam explicitly teaches its followers that Jesus was not God *"in the flesh"* or God's son but simply a man – a prophet of God, yes, but nothing more. We will see in the next section why it is essential that Jesus was not "just a man."

Muslims (the followers of Islam) do not believe Jesus was crucified or resurrected either in the same way that Jews do not. However, I am not lumping Jews and Muslims together as evil or deceived. Followers of other religions too cannot simply be lumped into one category or another because the entire picture is so very complicated.

Even atheists have their system of beliefs about how reality works, though, they recoil from calling non-belief a religion. Still, they do congregate in meetings and conventions to discuss and spread their beliefs and give each other support just as every other religious group does. I suppose that "free thinking" by yourself at home is quite lonely. I say that tongue-in-cheek, knowing full well the reality of things.

We are all more alike than dissimilar. Every one of us seeks out others who are like in mind for companionship and support. God made us social beings after all, so in dealing with all the different religions and viewpoints of the world, we must acknowledge our limited perspectives and submit to another command to us: Do not judge others.

Not only are there religions that are partially based on true reality, in which atheist beliefs are included, but there are also religions that have been created or infiltrated by agents of the ancient spiritual war (one can also argue that atheist beliefs are also tainted by those agents). The fact that people have spiritual experiences and encounters from religions around the world is no surprise then.

However, that alone doesn't give credence to one religion or another. It does further reinforce that a spiritual world exists. The real evidence for the Truth of the Big Picture is all the correlating data or empirical evidence, if you will, that aligns directly with Christianity. The first half of this book was devoted to that evidence.

How then with this complex schematic are we to proceed in applying religion and belief to our own lives? It is not our place to judge **people** because we do not know their complete circumstances nor do we know their hearts. Many people are simply born into a religion, including Christianity, and grow up in its culture without truly understanding its principles. We also cannot pester or coerce others into following our paths or believing the truth as we see it.

At most, we can share our experiences and make recommendations. It is up to the other person entirely whether they want to put that information to use. Instead, we should use the powers of intelligence that God gave us and consider what is most reasonable and logical. We *can* judge what is right and wrong in order to proceed on or correct the paths along our own life maps.

So in this way, I will not judge a Jew for not believing in Jesus, nor will I judge a Muslim for believing in altered scripture, nor will I judge a Buddhist for not believing in a God Creator. **However, I can judge their beliefs, statements, and evidence,** and point out the discrepancies I see in their viewpoints as it pertains to the Big Picture. I will do this as I have been doing all along in this book and then simply move on.

A Learning Process

Recall earlier when I talked about our confounding reality – that Satan, the serpent in Genesis, coaxed Eve into committing the original sin. However, Adam and Eve could not have committed the original sin if the tree of the knowledge of good and evil was not placed in the Garden of Eden in the first place.

God placed it there for a reason, as he does so many things, and told Adam and Eve not to eat from it as a test and so that the sin *could* be committed. God knew exactly what he was doing and what would happen. It was done in order that not just Adam and Eve could learn but humanity as a whole. Our learning process is the last but most important part of the Big Picture I will discuss here.

In the beginning, there was no Law decreed by God for Man other than, do not eat from the tree of the knowledge of good and evil. The Creation was *"good,"* he said. The stars were placed and the earth was formed. Our planet was sculpted further with an atmosphere, oceans, and geologic processes that we have only just begun to understand.

Then he made life sprout across all the globe and the earth became a truly living planet. Adam and Eve came last and were free from death and sin at this time. They were in a truly innocent and naive state. We do not know how long they lived in this state, but once they ate from the tree, which embodies all the rules of morality that God laid out for our reality, they were thrust into the fallen or sinful state in which we now live as a consequence. Some say they were punished for their actions, but it would be more accurate to say it was a method of teaching since God intended it as part of his master plan.

Humanity and our reality was put into a state corrupted by sin and death so that we could have that Free-State Reality, an existence that forces us to know how good the good is by having to know the bad. However, God initially let mankind progress on its own without much intervention or formal Law. There were only the universal moral laws that were embodied in the tree of the knowledge of good and evil. These are the "innate" and shared moral rules that every human has no matter what culture they are born to, such as murder is bad, helping others is good, oppressing others is bad, and so on. They are the moral rules in which our conscience uses to evaluate our options and behavior.

This was a period of almost unhindered free will for humans since there was very little punishment or direction by God at this time. It was a testing period for us to see how well we could fare on our own. About ten very long generations later (humans lived to almost 1000 years old at this time), though, we had made a mess of our free will privilege, just as undisciplined adolescents would do if given too much freedom.

Simply setting the rules of morality was not enough to make most people lead a life of righteousness. The passions of our blood simmered without restraint. All those little bubbles carried the sin from the heat in our hearts outward into the world, and our sinful natures kept surfacing without punishment to distract us.

The dark forces in the spiritual war were active as well, urging us further into deviant behavior, and so at this time *"The Lord saw how great man's wickedness on the earth had become, and that every inclination of the thoughts of his heart was only evil all the time."* Genesis 6:5. Justice had to be maintained by God's standards and so he brought the Flood to cleanse mankind and the earth of the sin inflicting them. This punishment was the first in an effort to discipline mankind as a whole.

God only spared Noah and his family to repopulate the earth. This allowed mankind to continue on but it also made witnesses to the disciplinary measure, so from the descendents of Noah the story of the Great Flood was handed down by tradition as a reminder of judgment for wrongdoing. This is how so many of the world's cultures can share a common flood mythology. All of us descended from Noah's family line, who witnessed the Flood.

As mankind recovered from its punishment and repopulated the earth, the next stage of God's plan in teaching us was put into effect. He would create a nation, a chosen people, to represent him and his best interests to the rest of the world. He chose one man, Abraham, to be the father of this nation, which eventually came to be called Israel.

Unlike Noah, who God considered righteous and blameless, there was nothing truly special about Abraham other than God chose him to father the chosen nation. This alludes to an important message that we will talk about in the next chapter.

Now God was working to create and nurture a chosen people, but why? The Coercion Factor. God couldn't keep coming down or sending angels to apply discipline and justice everywhere as we saw him do many times in the Old Testament. He needed human representatives on earth to know, apply, and teach his Law. This is an extremely important responsibility for these people because they were representing God himself and the overall good he intended for the whole of mankind.

This premier role for the Israelites was one reason why God gave them so many strict rules of conduct, rituals of cleansing from all types of sin, and harsh punishments for crime among them. He even gave them rules for hygiene to help quarantine and limit the spread of infectious diseases, which was over a thousand years before science came to the same conclusions after the discovery of how bacteria and viruses spread.

All of the strict rules for the Israelites were not just to make them as holy or close to God as possible or to protect them, but they were also meant to test them. Testing us is a persistent feature in mankind's learning process and in the next chapter we will see that God continues to test us as individuals as well.

For the Israelites, God had come down and shown them miracles and powers beyond imagination as he guided and forged them into the chosen nation. He brought plagues into Egypt and freed them from slavery. He provided for them over the span of decades in the desert and helped them conquer the land that was promised to them.

However, the Israelites were people just like you and me, prone to failure and forgetting. As generations passed, the miracles witnessed by previous generations faded and God's Law was often forgotten or overlooked. As a result, the Israelites committed the same unholy things as the other nations and were punished for it many times.

The Bible is full of judgment and punishment for the Israelites as well as other nations, but God knew the nature of man and had planned from the beginning how to deal with it. His master plan to teach mankind was unfolding and he would not continue to just let the cycle of sinning and punishing continue endlessly.

Through his most trusted and devoted servants, the Israelite prophets or messengers of God, he told them that someone was coming to free them from all the oppressions of the world, a savior messiah, and laid out exactly how they could recognize him. He seemed to tell them everything they needed to know except when the savior was coming.

In their more worldly and limited understanding of the message, though, many Israelites thought the messiah would simply be a king or leader who would free them from the oppression of other nations. God had much bigger plans than that.

He was planning a way out of oppression for all of mankind, not just for the Israelites. The role of the Israelites was to represent God through history, to record and preserve His Law and their testimony as to the true nature of reality through His Word in the Bible. The Israelites would be the vehicle that would launch the mechanism to save mankind, and the kind of oppression we would be saved from was not from rulers, tyrants, or nations, but from ourselves.

God knew our nature from the start. That sin lived within us and it was a powerful force that we could not control without his help. On its own, it made us satisfy biological desires and urges, such as lust and rage, and other bad products of a Free-State Reality, like pride and greed, but in conjunction with the opposing forces of the spiritual war we succumbed far too easily to short-sighted, self gratifying behavior. The carrots dangling in front of us were too appetizing, the frosting on the cakes too delectable, and so we sprung the traps over and over again.

We needed something to snap us out of the trance induced by our hearts' desires and instinctual programming. The mechanism that God would deliver to us through the line of his chosen people –

through the Savior he was sending – would be something called Grace. It stems out of his love for us and blooms as an elegant way to subdue the thorns of our sinful nature.

He knew all of us would fall to sin one way or another, so instead of preventing it entirely and binding our hands and minds with punishment after punishment, he would forgive it. It was a gift of mercy born straight from his omnibenevolence, and he would grant it if only we would simply acknowledge Him and sincerely repent – realize our wrongdoing, apologize, and change.

Why these terms for Grace? As a fully sentient person, God wants to be acknowledged just as anyone else does. Who wants to go about life being completely ignored, especially by those you love? Or worse, who wants to be demeaned and dejected by those you value?

God simply wants our acknowledgment just as any loving parent would want from their children. However, through much of our history, Man, the children he created, had rejected him. There are different reasons for this but the most direct factor is that God works subtly. He does not want to coerce belief.

Then repentance… we had wronged God by not acknowledging him and going against his best intentions for us. All of us would want an apology in the same kind of situation. The power to heal that a simple apology gives to both parties is worth much more than the inconvenience of humbling yourself or hurting your pride. The power of reconciliation can mend arguments and feuds that are centuries old.

God knows this power is far greater than showing a firm hand and stout back, so he humbles himself to us by offering his unfettered mercy. But we must also humble ourselves to accept it. If we do not bend our knees in acceptance of God and his ways, then we are not humbling ourselves but being false about it. It is our continuing actions that truly show our hearts intentions, and that is why God wants us to change as we move forward from the initial apology.

Grace is a simple and elegant mechanism, but like God's other elegant devices, such as DNA and superstrings, implementing it would be much more difficult. We are willful children, so how could he get us to acknowledge him and repent without coercion?

This is where Jesus comes in and why it is so **absolutely** important that he is not simply a man or prophet. Jesus Christ was and is God himself. He wrote himself into our story as Jesus, came down to our level as the Son of God so we could understand him by our ways of seeing the world. He also made sure that it was clear he was not just a son but truly an extension of God, another part of himself. Through Jesus, God allows us to relate to Him directly and thereby acknowledge him, satisfying the first term for Grace.

Acknowledgment was not the only thing he wanted, though. To be truly obedient and graced children, we also needed to sincerely repent – to realize we had been wrong, apologize to him, and also strive to correct ourselves in the future. Again though, how would he get that message across without showing his strong arm? Only wisdom can take the place of might and overpower strength, and so the strong fires burning inside us because of sin would be squelched by the power of lightning from heaven.

God devised a powerful and passionate message for us out of his wisdom. The message would come through the things that Jesus did. It wasn't all the miracles he performed, all the healing, raising of the dead, and displays of supernatural power. These were only signs of his true nature, his omnipotence, and a reinforcement to us that he was indeed God. No, the critical thing he did was to make himself an example to us – the perfect example of how to attain Grace through sinless life, through acknowledging God, through obedience, and through sacrifice.

Jesus led a truly sinless life as only God could do. He, the Son, also acknowledged God, the Father, and was a completely obedient child. So obedient, in fact, that he went straight to the most excruciating death of the time (crucifixion) despite expressing fear of it the night before.

Then Jesus went with his disciples to a place called Gethsemane, and he said to them, "Sit here while I go over there and pray." He took Peter and the two sons of Zebedee along with him, and he began to be sorrowful and troubled. Then he said to them, "My soul is overwhelmed with sorrow to the point of death. Stay here and keep watch with me."

Going a little farther, he fell with his face to the ground and prayed, "My Father, if it is possible, may this cup be taken from me. Yet not as I will, but as you will."

...He went a second time and prayed, "My Father, if it is not possible for this cup to be taken away unless I drink it, may your will be done."

...So he left them again and went away once more and prayed the third time, saying the same thing.
Matthew 26:36

Jesus was human at the time and so naturally expressed fear of his death. He prayed three times that God, the Father, release him from his duty. However, Jesus also knew the answer to those prayers and exactly what his purpose on earth was, so in complete obedience he took and drank the cup symbolizing God's wrath towards the sins of mankind. It meant going to his death for all of humanity, for us, to atone for all our wrongdoing throughout history. God sacrificed His Son (Himself) for our sake even though he had done no wrong.

He was innocent of all wrongdoing yet as a loving parent, he sacrificed his life in order for his children to continue on in a better way. This was an act of pure love and mercy as well as another example for us to follow. Not an example to die literally, but to be freed from sin and live spiritually because Jesus was resurrected after his death, completely renewed and, literally, a shining example of how we too can be healed of the oppression from sin. I copy a part of my Easter sermon from my testimony here to note this:

For that is why Jesus died and rose again. It was an act of sacrifice and rebirth, both literal and symbolic to make absolutely clear His message to us – that we too must sacrifice and be reborn.

This sacrifice and rebirth is another absolutely important aspect of implementing Grace and why we must believe that Jesus was resurrected in order to receive it. God made a New Covenant with us on that day of his symbolic death – a new Law for all of mankind:

I will put my laws in their minds and write them on their hearts. I will be their God, and they will be my people. No longer will a man teach his neighbor, or a man his brother, saying, "Know the Lord," because they will all know me, from the least of them to the greatest. For I will forgive their wickedness and will remember their sins no more. Hebrews 8:10

The New Covenant of living under Grace completely replaced the old in which the Israelites were given through Moses. It would free them from all the strict rules and regulations made to purify and test them, and at the same time for everyone (not just the Israelites), it would free us all from the judgment and punishment cycle and put within reach the ultimate reward created for all of mankind since the beginning of time – the Kingdom of Heaven – and fellowship with God.

It would make God accessible to every one of us – to know him personally (*"they will all know me"*) and show us his infinite faith and love for us through mercy (*"I will forgive their wickedness and will remember their sins no more"*). How can a god that is not omnibenevolent offer such grand and overarching benevolence? He was offering forgiveness for ANY and ALL wrongs we have done.

All we need to do is accept the terms for Grace – acknowledge God through Jesus Christ (believe wholeheartedly in him and what he did *"in the flesh"*) and sincerely repent. It couldn't be any simpler, but in actuality, those are just the first steps into the light of Grace. Grace is not like a "go free card" to do anything we wish, ask for forgiveness, and repeat. God decreed Grace as the new Law by which we should live, but the effort is not his alone.

We must also implement Grace in our own lives, in our minds, and in our hearts – change ourselves to align with God's best intentions. To do that we must follow Christ (God) by the example he set in Jesus. This will be the focus of the next chapter, but we're not quite finished here.

The next chapter focuses on our individual learning process, but mankind's learning process continues as well. God had told Israel the Savior, Jesus, was coming hundreds of years before he came, and we see throughout Biblical history that significant time spans elapse between stages of God's plan. In fact, I believe we are nearing one of the next stages of mankind's learning process, some two thousand years after the time of Jesus. Why the significant time spans? Is God on holiday during all of this "down time?" Of course not.

The time scales are not for God's benefit. They're for ours because as limited beings we need time to grow and learn. For example, we cannot just write a story from birth. We must learn words and grammar first, then we can learn the tools of writing and storytelling. In this way, humanity itself needs to evolve before certain stages of the learning process can take place.

An example of this is when Jesus was asked about divorce, *"Is it lawful for a man to divorce his wife for any and every reason?"* Matthew 19:3 because under the Old Covenant divorce was allowed if the wife *"becomes displeasing"* to the husband because *"he finds something indecent about her."* Deuteronomy 24:1, which can be interpreted broadly.

Jesus replied, "Moses permitted you to divorce your wives because your hearts were hard. But it was not this way from the beginning. I tell you that anyone who divorces his wife, except for marital unfaithfulness, and marries another woman commits adultery." Matthew 19:8.

Jesus meant that broader terms for divorce were given in the time of Moses because their *"hearts were hard"* – they were not ready or mature enough for the Law that God intended from the beginning, which was that man and woman are not to divorce at all unless one of them are unfaithful.

Their hearts were too rigid, too stubborn, and their minds too set in their own ways to accept the ideal. We were simply not ready for many of the things God wanted for the greater good. And to this day, many of us are still not ready.

However, the beauty of Grace is that we do not have to be ready for everything that God wants for us all at once. He knows we will make mistakes and is willing to forgive them, but he also won't stop there. He promised us healing as well – *"I have seen his willful ways, but I will heal him; I will guide him and restore comfort to him."* Isaiah 57:18.

God will help us change ourselves so that we are ready for what he wants of us, and how he does this is in a way that highlights another reason why our reality is so confoundingly constructed against the prideful.

Humility was mentioned before as a virtue opposing Pride and to submit to the terms of Grace is also to humble yourself before God. However, there is another virtue that opposes Pride. It is a virtue we will fully discuss in the next chapter and is the means by which God's promised healing comes. It is Faith – belief in God despite his invisibility in our lives, despite what science tells us, despite what the world tells us, and despite everything else that says he does not exist.

God is perfect in nature and logic, and the master of multi-layered communication and symbolism. He crossed every T and dotted every I. He filled in all the blanks to make reality appear as if it and we did not need him, but the truth is, in the great vastness of our universe, in the invisible, intangible nature of the spiritual realm, and in his very subtle ways, our Lord whispers a simple message:

There is more...

There is more to our reality.
There is more to our lives.
There is more to us.
There is more to God.

Following the Compass

Love is the motivation,
Faith the means, and
Fellowship the reward.

*T*hat is the simplest summary and most important message of the whole last chapter, the Big Picture of Reality – the "Why?" for our existence and reality's multi-layered and confusing nature. God created us out of Love, he built reality to redeem Faith, and the reward is Fellowship with Him in heaven. However, Faith is not just believing in God. He declared the mechanism, Law, or New Covenant for us to take the necessary steps into Faith and called it Grace. It was delivered and is provided by Jesus Christ, God's extension of "The Son" enabling us all to personally interact with him.

The terms of Grace were given to all of mankind so that we may be freed from the consequences of sin, but it is on an individual basis that Grace is accepted and applied. This chapter will focus wholly on that individual acceptance and subsequent transformation provided by Grace. You may wonder though, "Why do I need Grace? Why do I even need God? I'm just not a religious person and perfectly happy with my life without all of this spiritualism."

There is more...

We ended the last chapter on the note of "more." There is more to us and our existence than can be seen with a superficial glance. We are made of more than atoms and chemical reactions, more than muscle, blood, and bone, and in fact, our whole reality is much more than what we can see on the surface. We are actually spiritual beings like the angels except that we are confined to a physical experience in this life, and to ignore the spiritual part of ourselves would be conceding to a much more limited and meaningless existence – that of only a physical nature, no better or worse than the animals of the world.

When we ignore our spiritual side, we actually starve and mute it like a gifted musician who never practices or plays. The harmony of melody will never be fully realized and the gift in us dries up. Furthermore, conceding to a meaningless existence not only excludes you from the "more" in your present life, but also in the next life. The one after death in which your spiritual self continues. Unlike the musician whose art may stagnant and crust over, never to awaken after so many ages, our spiritual side can never truly die and can be renewed fully. It may have dried up and shriveled, but it remains thirsty and ready to accept the water it needs to grow.

"If anyone is thirsty, let him come to me and drink. Whoever believes in me, as the Scripture has said, streams of living water will flow from within him." John 7:37. Jesus said this to emphasize that he is the key to composing our symphonies. Belief in Him, in God, will quench our spiritual thirst and enable us to grow with an ample supply of water – the spiritual water I introduced in Chapter Three – the Holy Spirit.

God created us to be much more than the animals, more than we can see with our eyes and understand from our perspectives. He wants us to understand and grow, though, and so he put in place a learning process for us, for humanity, to learn about and appreciate the life given to us. In that process, the first step was to make the world fall to sin in order that not only free will be given or that we could know the good by knowing the bad but to test us. *"But the Scripture declares that the whole world is a prisoner of sin..."* Galatians 3:22

Many people do not realize this fallen nature to the world and that we are born slaves into it. There is so much more to our existence if you realize that the shackles inherent in sin can be broken. You can be freed from the corruption and pain of this world and be set on the path that will bring true, perfect happiness.

Not the "perfect" that you envision in your mind's eye, but the one that God sees. He knows us completely – what we desire and what makes us most joyful. His omniscience sees that, and because of his omnibenevolence, he desires the very best for us. That "very best" may be a path in life you never would have imagined, so no matter how good you think you have it without God, it cannot be measured to how good it can be with God.

Being right with God or in fellowship with him is not the same thing as being religious. When most people think of "religious," they think of superstition, they think of ritual, and they think of conformity or submission. All very unpopular notions in today's highly independent and scientific society, but try not to fall to Selective Reasoning. We have been taught those notions by the "world" – by our culture, the media, and that Blob – and they are very attractive things that feed our selfish desires to do as we please and think as we please. Christianity, though, is not about superstition but explains the supernatural, and it is not about rituals but frees us from being enslaved robots. However, it *is* about submission, not to society or the church, but to God himself.

You may be afraid to submit to an all powerful, all knowing God. After all, what if you do something wrong and then God smites you with a bolt from on high? Figuratively, of course, but you can't help having the image of a cartoon character being fried crispy, standing there smoldering, and thinking, "What just happened?" As amusing as that may seem, the truth is, God does not want us to live in fear. Recall the Coercion Factor and the First and Greatest Commandment from the last chapter.

God, being omnipotent, has every right to enforce his laws in any way he wishes, and if he did not want more from us then we would already have been done "extra crispy" many times over. God is omnibenevolent not punitive and wise not rash. He wants a more meaningful relationship with us than that of master and servant or king and subject. He wants us to acknowledge and be in fellowship with him as loving parent and loving child. It is in that relationship he can be our Compass and guide us along our life maps towards our greater good.

If we continue with Galatians 3:22, *"...the whole world is a prisoner of sin, so that what was promised, being given through faith in Jesus Christ, might be given to those who believe."* It says the world was put in sin so we could be rewarded through faith in God – through faith in Jesus Christ. The bricks in the foundation of reality were stacked and mortared in a way to confound the prideful – to test and filter those who would rather not acknowledge God but believe in their own conclusions and devices. That test is Faith and we all must step through that filter in order to go to the next level of fellowship with God.

The First Small Step

Our first step into fellowship with God is to step into his offer of Grace and acknowledge him. To do this and begin our journey through the filter of Faith, just as with most physical filters, we must become small to go through the strainer – humble ourselves to God by acknowledging him through Jesus Christ. All this means is believing in him and what he did – that he does exist now, was here on earth *"in the flesh"* as Jesus, was killed on the cross for our benefit, and resurrected in triumph.

This first step can be difficult because of our attitudes toward religion, spiritualism, and superstition. After all, how often do we acknowledge an invisible, intangible person as here and alive with us right now, especially someone who did some very supernatural things so long ago? Not since the first grade, you may quip, but Jesus is not an imaginary friend.

As young children, we may have believed in imaginary friends and had all sorts of play with them through the creativity of our minds, but Jesus, not being imaginary nor solely an internal entity, can interact with us in ways you never thought possible. Our witness testimonies in Chapters Three and Four showed the nature of this interaction, so if you are ready to take the first step through Faith, all you need to do is find a quiet place, close your eyes for focus, bow your head to show submission, clasp your hands together to show respect, and then simply pray to him.

You may think, but I don't know how to pray. Most people start out this way, at a loss for words and apprehensive. I certainly did. First time, my words fumbled and I mumbled, but I made the effort to be whole-hearted and sincere. That is most important so don't worry about fumbling, just make the effort.

Eventually, you will find that praying is no different than speaking to someone important to you, one-on-one. Simply talk to God as you would anyone else you respect. Address him by his name, Jesus Christ, and title, Lord, and go from there. There needs to be no ritual about it. Just give him your heart and mind and speak with him.

Smaller Still

The next part in accepting Grace is to repent – to become smaller still, admit you were wrong, and strive to correct yourself in the future. During your first prayer state your apologies to him and ask for forgiveness for all your sins. State your more major or recent mistakes specifically as well.

Being specific is always better because even though God knows all we have done, it shows our ownership for our mistakes – that we are willing to take responsibility for them. Which apology sounds more sincere? "Please forgive me for that thing I did last week," or "Please, Lord, forgive me for losing my temper and lashing out at my wife."

And remember that sin is anything (thought, speech, or action) that opposes God's will or Law – anything that takes us further away from perfect fellowship with him. In that way, every single one of us has sinned and will continue to sin through our lives. It is our nature and the nature of our world, so repentance and fighting sin will be ongoing activities for all of us no matter how long we have followed Christ.

Jesus pointed this out when people brought a woman caught in adultery to him and asked him to judge and condemn her according to Jewish law (death by stoning). He responded, *"If any one of you is without sin, let him be the first to throw a stone at her."* John 8:7. At that remark the group slowly dispersed without one stone being thrown.

Everyone realized they were no "cleaner" than the accused woman, so even if you think that you have done horrible things and are undeserving of Grace, realize that all of us are imperfect, all of us have made mistakes, and all of us have drifted away at one time or another from the ideal set by Jesus. God knows this and yet accepts us **no**

matter what we have done.

After the crowd went away from the woman and Jesus, he asked her,

"Woman, where are they? Has no one condemned you?"

"No one, sir," she said.

"Then neither do I condemn you," Jesus declared. "Go now and leave your life of sin." John 8:10

He accepted her in sin and he will accept every one of us in the same way. It does not matter what we have done. All we need do is sincerely apologize and strive for a sinless life (repent), just as he commanded the woman after he forgave her, *"Go now and leave your life of sin."*

In Ezekiel 16, God relates how abhorrent the sins of Israel had been since he freed them from slavery in Egypt and built them up as a rich and powerful nation in the days of King David and King Solomon. Their sins were so bad that they eclipsed the wrongs of previous generations. Everything from sexual immorality to the sacrifice of first-born children had subverted God's will.

His chosen people turned their backs on him a million times over, yet out of his omnibenevolence, out of his infinite capacity for mercy, he promised a last chance for them through a new everlasting covenant – the New Covenant called Grace. Jesus delivered this new agreement as promised, but it was not just meant to wash the sins of the Israelites. It was for all of mankind to atone for our mistakes.

We do not need to be from a certain background, ethnicity, or country nor do we need to have special abilities, a "pure" heart, or anything else for God to grant us Grace. All of us can agree to his offer exactly in line with what he told Apostle Paul, *"I have made you a light for the Gentiles, that you may bring salvation to the ends of the earth."* Acts 13:47. Gentiles were anyone who was not a Jew and so in that statement God declared that Grace was for everyone and not just for the chosen nation of Israel.

My own calling into Grace highlights this as well. I am a regular person just as you are, was brought up without religion, embraced the freedoms of our age, and have committed many regretful things in my years, yet God made it clear to me that he offered Grace, and when I accepted, he nurtured me into and through Faith. He will do exactly the same for you.

Signing the New Covenant

The third and final step into Grace is to "formally" accept his offer. This is a small but critical step. Overlooking it or doing it incorrectly will keep your name from being entered into the Book of Life – God's book that holds the names of everyone who have successfully secured their salvation.

The proper way of accepting Grace has been misunderstood for centuries as the church has distorted His Word with so many different viewpoints and interpretations. This is a serious problem that was brought to my attention by the revelations of Pastor Roy Sauzek. The supplement to this book, *Messages from the 3rd Compass* (available free at 3rdCompass.com), discusses this issue more fully, but here I will only discuss how God requires us to accept Grace as he decreed, for Jesus said in Matthew 10:32:

Whoever acknowledges me before men, I will also acknowledge him before my Father in heaven. But whoever disowns me before men, I will disown him before my Father in heaven.

These two statements sounds straightforward. It sounds like we only need to show outwardly that we believe in Jesus and not keep our faith internal to be admitted to heaven, correct? Look closer. Wring every bit of Truth out of His Word to understand it completely.

Note, there are only two statements – no in between conditions. Therefore, you can fulfill only one condition or the other. That is a matter of simple logic, which means skipping your formal acceptance of Grace results in the same consequence as disowning or denying Jesus – you are barred from entering heaven.

We want to fulfill the first statement then, but what does *"Whoever acknowledges me before men..."* really mean? Let us turn to His Word again and to someone who truly understood what Jesus meant. Apostle Paul said:

The word is near you; it is in your mouth and in your heart, that is, the word of faith we are proclaiming: That if you confess with your mouth, "Jesus is Lord," and believe in your heart that God raised him from the dead, you will be saved. For it is with your heart that you believe and are justified, and it is with your mouth that you confess and are saved. Romans 10:8

Paul makes it clear to us Jesus meant that we must confess our belief in Christ by our mouth and heart. That is the acknowledgement Jesus was referring to in Matthew 10:32, but he also qualifies that acknowledgement with *"before men."* This means the final step in accepting Grace is to confess your belief in Jesus ***"before men"*** or **in the presence of others (face-to-face) with your mouth and heart** (personal conviction).

The *"before men"* qualifier means that speaking on the telephone, writing a letter, sending an email or any other form of remote communication does not qualify as an acceptance of Grace by God's terms. God wants our confession to be in the direct presence of another. After all, how do we communicate with God? We pray, don't we? We don't send him emails or write giant letters in the sand so that he can see them in heaven. We speak to him directly. God witnesses our prayers personally, and in the same way, he wants a witness on earth for our agreement to Grace.

Now we know what to do, but how do we do it? Paul gives an example above in Romans 10:8. You don't need to make a speech about it. All you need say is, "Jesus is Lord," to someone, and if you truly believe in His Gospel (that Jesus died for our sins and that he was resurrected) then you are saved or "born again." Your name is entered into the Book of Life at the very moment.

Another way that you may fulfill this step of confession is the same way that I did. During my baptism, my pastor asked me, "Do you believe Jesus died for your sins and God raised Him from the dead?"

I answered, "Yes."

And that is it. One or two words from your mouth in the presence of another person that affirm your belief in Jesus. It can be an answer to a question (the drawing of a confession) or a statement that you bring out yourself (straight confession). The important thing is that it comes from your heart. This means repeating a "repeat after me" statement does not fulfill the confession requirement of the New Covenant.

If someone says, "Repeat after me... I believe Jesus died for my sins and God raised Him from the dead," and you say it, the statement did not come from your heart. You only repeated a statement like a tape recorder. The words entered your ears and then went straight back out through your mouth. Your heart (decision making process) was bypassed. This detail may seem dogmatic and nitpicky, but God declared His Law this way for a reason.

Grace is a covenant or holy agreement between you and Him. You are making a promise to Him and Him to you. He wants us to actively make a decision to accept this contract. It is that important, so he requires us to generate our statement of confession from the heart. And he requires it to be in the physical presence of at least one other person, not only that he may be witness, but also as an act of humility – for the terms of accepting Grace mirror the First and Second Commandments.

Your belief in Jesus and His Gospel fulfill the First Commandment, "Love the Lord" and humbles you before God. Your confession to another person fulfills the Second Commandment, "Love your neighbor," and humbles you before your fellow human. *All the Law and the Prophets hang on these two commandments,* Matthew 23:37, and so the terms for accepting Grace synch with this thinking.

It couldn't be any easier for us. All we need to do is sincerely believe in Jesus Christ and what he did, repent, and accept his promise. Those are the first steps into Faith. You don't have to meditate for hours or give your blood or sacrifice a bull or chicken. God wants everyone to have easy access, and what could be easier than talking to him right where you are?

Once you have accepted your belief in Jesus and humbled yourself to God through prayer, commit yourself to fulfilling the terms of confessing your faith. Your commitment to Grace is not signed until you have made your confession, so go to a friend, family, or church member and admit your belief in Christ.

Now, you might not notice anything new or changed after your first prayer or confession of belief, but God will notice. The change comes little by little as you continue along through the filter of Faith. Accepting Grace is like casting off a heavy, stained and moth eaten coat. It is the decayed covering that sin smothers our spiritual self with. It restricts our movements and darkens our hearts, but once it is thrown away our limbs can move freely and the light can shine through.

Throwing the coat away allows us to reach out for that promised treasure, *"a treasure in heaven that will not be exhausted, where no thief comes near and no moth destroys,"* Luke 12:33. Then we can continue forward to fellowship with God by living in Grace.

Tools of Faith

Before we continue, though, we need to look at the tools that are necessary on your journey through Faith. The first is God's Word, the Holy Bible. Like a field guide for an adventurer in rough and unknown terrain, the Bible is an essential guide for navigating reality. My testimony in Chapter Three highlighted its importance as a tool for guidance and in Chapter Five I stated it was also given to us as a standard and measure – to judge and discern what is in alignment with God and what is not.

Besides being in direct communication with God as the prophets, saints, and apostles were, there is no other way to judge what is right and wrong in God's eyes than to know and understand His Word in the Bible, so it is critical to apply it in context and in entirety. The Big Picture cannot be framed with twisted, omitted, or changed Scripture.

To equip yourself through Faith then, get a Bible, one that uses modern English at first so that God's Word comes through clearer, like the New International Version (NIV), because older Bibles, such as the King James Version, use language that is uncommon and outdated, which can confuse your reading.

If possible, get a Study Bible that has academic notes along with the Scripture so that you can understand context better. In Chapter Five, I noted how important it is to know and understand Scripture in proper context (the Spirit of the Word) and not read it strictly literally (the Letter of the Word).

Reading the Bible and trying to understand God on your own, though, can be very difficult, so the next tool you need to guide you through Faith is the church and other experts on interpreting and understanding God and His Word. Read books about Faith and Christianity. Find a church, go to services, and enroll in a study group for new believers. It is a great help and comfort to be aided by others who are on the same journey as you. Not only that, but God created mankind to work as a body with different members having different capabilities so that we may help one another through our life journeys.

Just as each of us has one body with many members, and these members do not all have the same function, so in Christ we who are many form one body, and each member belongs to all the others. Romans 12:4

This body is called the Body of Christ, which is essentially "the church," but it is not the building, the place of worship, the minister, or the people who run the church. It is all of us, all of those living under Grace, so don't be afraid to ask anyone else in the Body for aid, advice, and comfort.

Remember that we have been all put here to not just be in fellowship with God but also each other – *"Love your neighbor as yourself."* And if asking for help in person is uncomfortable for you then you may want to try other resources, such as the Internet. There are many Christian web sites that can provide information, discussion, and consoling. Check to see if your church has web services or you may also go to www.3rdCompass.com for further help and resources.

The last tool you need in Faith is prayer. Praying activates the connection we have with God and builds it up, filling us more and more with the Holy Spirit – the living water that our spirit needs to thrive. Praying is the means he wants us to speak with him and by doing it we also build our personal relationship with him. It helps maintain our fellowship with God and strengthens Faith, so pray often and for anything.

Living in Grace

We have accepted the agreement with God (Grace) and arranged our tools within reach to continue along our journey. We are now ready to live in Grace and have God himself, guide and transform our lives. The transformation will not come overnight, and in fact will continue through the rest of our lives, but little by little, one small step at a time, the changes of going through the filter of Faith will not just redirect the paths along our life maps but also reform our very selves.

This redirection reprograms us and bypasses our instinctual programming, biological wiring, and cultural/societal dispositions so that we can align with God's ultimate goal and place for us by his side in the kingdom of heaven – an immortal life where ideal morality and a truly good existence can be realized. In our "natural," sinful states, we are not ready for such an existence because we are truly immature beings driven more by selfish, instinctual desires than by the perfect logic and morality that God envisions.

"As for God, his way is perfect; the word of the Lord is flawless." 2 Samuel 22:31. We must realize that and follow in the guidance set by His Word as well as the guidance he gives to each of us individually. You can think of this guidance as an advanced lifestyle and morality school – the individual learning process that parallels the learning process given to mankind as a whole – and when we graduate from this life the glowing treasure of the Lord's Kingdom is tied as the tassel to our cap and gown.

A Time for Everything

However, like going through college, our learning process will take time and can be difficult, so it is important to embrace one of His first lessons. It was a lesson I was reminded of during my own guidance as I often questioned God, "When?" When will things happen? When will my life change? When can I expect this or that? I was and still am like a kid on a trip to the candy story. I keep asking when I will get there, and when I do, what delicious confections will I have? The licorice, the sour balls, the taffy, or, oh, my favorite, dark chocolate anything! His answer to me was always the same though – Have patience.

There is a time for everything,
and a season for every activity under heaven:
a time to be born and a time to die,
a time to plant and a time to uproot,
a time to kill and a time to heal,
a time to tear down and a time to build,
a time to mourn and a time to dance,
a time to scatter stones and a time to gather them,
a time to embrace and a time to refrain,
a time to search and a time to give up,
a time to keep and a time to throw away,
a time to tear and a time to mend,
a time to be silent and a time to speak,
a time to love and a time to hate,
a time for war and a time for peace. Ecclesiastes 3:1

There is a proper time for everything and so we must quiet our hearts and be patient. Stay your surging heart and don't expect everything to happen all at once. Significant breakthroughs in your learning process may take months or even years, but realize that as you continue along, every small step forward in Faith brings you closer to your desired destination. Changes in my own life took many months before I could see that I and it had indeed changed significantly since the time I began.

We may have our own ideas of how things should work and how long they should take, but God has his plans already laid out, and it is not just "a plan" but it is the ideal plan for us as a whole and for us as individuals. He has that capacity to weave our lives through and with one another for the greater good. Put your trust in that. Put your trust in his love for us and his perfect sense of benevolence.

The times he has set for things to happen are for reason and they may be far off of what we might expect or want. After all, it took decades for the Israelites to reach their promised land and centuries for Jesus to deliver Grace after God had promised these things. Fortunately, the time spans in our lives are much shorter, but realize that many things will take time. Consider it a test of Faith to wait on his promises patiently.

Another lesson to embrace from Ecclesiastes 3 is that there is an appropriate time for everything. Many people view Christianity as a shackle to bind our lives in melancholy submission – that we should not be passionate or show feelings – but nothing could be further than the truth.

God created us to feel and have true emotions, but he does not want our emotions to control our behavior. Doing so would be submitting to our instinctual programming that can lead very swiftly into sin, such as feeling anger and resentment drives us to hate and persecute or satisfying lust, greed and pride drives us into meaningless sexual relationships.

We are not mere animals so that we should go about our lives simply satisfying biological cravings, nor are we here to simply survive. We were created to be more and better, so exercise restraint in all you do. Filter your thoughts and actions by God's ideals. Ask yourself, how would Jesus go about this?

Restraint doesn't mean becoming an emotionless robot. It means having discipline as Jesus did. He was full of emotion. He had passion and showed anger when appropriate, but not once did he let emotions control him. He never struck or belittled someone in anger nor did he fall to biological cravings and pursue sex or marriage. Jesus was completely disciplined, but he showed love and passion for so many things. He knew exactly that *there is a time for everything.*

God embodied himself in Jesus so that he could set the perfect example for us to follow. Only God, though, could do it perfectly and lead a truly sinless life. The rest of us struggle in the battles with sin, but that does not mean we should raise the white flag and surrender to it, conceding that we are just not good enough to follow God's example.

Doing that would be overlooking the Big Picture because God came as Jesus for more than to set an example. He came to offer his help. He knows we cannot be as perfect as him, so he extends his hand to us through Grace in order that we can accept his help and follow him.

Embrace his hand to embrace Grace and the life he gave to us. By all means, show love and passion in all you do, but do it righteously just as Jesus did – in a way that is right in God's eyes. One can be angry at a wrong, but don't harbor resentment and vengeance. Instead, forgive and try to right the wrong in an agreeable way. One can have pride in a job well done, but don't fall to the sin of Pride and be boastful or belittling to others. Accept victories with humility and conduct affairs with honor. One can have passionate relations inside a marriage, but outside marriage all sexual activities must be deferred.

In fact, patronage for all things like pornography, strip clubs, and prostitution that misconstrue and distort God's purposes for sex must be taken away. A "new age," freedom loving society may view Christian philosophy about sex as prudish, but realize that these ideals were given by an omniscient God who can see the outcome of every action and attitude. You may not think that looking at pornography or taking part in consensual, premarital sex hurts anyone, but that would be viewing reality from our limited perspectives – more Selective Reasoning.

God can see the entire picture – that in producing pornography and running brothels people are violated and taken advantage of, that making sex merely a biological satisfaction also makes people mere objects or toys to be played with, that sex without true love embodied by marriage sends a message to our children that quick and easy gratification is better than discipline, patience, and love.

Those are only the most obvious side-effects of sexual immorality. There is much more going on than we can see and understand, so we must acknowledge that when we consider God's instruction on any matter and put trust in his greater wisdom.

Issues of anger, sex and pride are relatively easy to understand, but we are confronted with choices of action in all sorts of situations where it may be unclear what the righteous path should be. To know what is right, we must know and understand God. This is why knowing and understanding His Word in the Bible is important. It is the main avenue he gave us to understand him, so to know and understand His Word is to know and understand Him.

As you continue along in Faith, make it a daily activity to read and understand the Bible so that when you ask, "What would Jesus do in my place?" you can answer with confidence. This is also why going to church and listening to sermons is important.

Insights can be gained from others that you may miss when you are studying alone. Of course, it takes time to absorb and understand His Word so when in doubt, consult with more experienced resources, such as your pastor, minister, church, and friends. The entire Body of Christ is at your side.

Listening to God

"And without faith it is impossible to please God, because anyone who comes to him must believe that he exists and that he rewards those who earnestly seek him." Hebrews 11:6

This leads us to the next lesson for living in Grace – How to listen to God's personal guidance for you. Recall the story in Chapter One, "Passing Signs," about the couple with an ill-fated marriage. Many signs or signals were passed to them, but they were oblivious to make the connection with the message God was trying to send – that they should not get married.

The "signs" came to them in the form of extremely "bad luck" with anything to do with the wedding, but how can we know for certain what are truly signs and what is just plain bad luck or mere coincidence? How can we know what are nudgings of the Holy Spirit and what are just desires from our own hearts?

The truth is, we cannot know for certain, 100%, that it is God speaking to us. Remember the role of Faith, though. It is not just a filter to strip Pride away. God also uses it to teach at the same time he guides. It would be far too easy for us if God just straight up, told us exactly what we needed to do. That is like asking your dorm roommate to give you the answers to a calculus test. Going straight to the answers bypasses the learning process and we are left without the understanding of how to work through problems and appreciating how the problems are solved.

The best we can do is listen with faith. Pay attention to things that "click" or speak to you in the moment. Listening to your gut or intuition may sound unscientific and illogical, but remember that the nature of God's interaction with us is 99% of the time very subtle. The reasons for this are the Coercion Factor and an important topic of this chapter – Faith. God wants us to build faith in his relationship with us, and so he will use Faith to do it. It is through trust in what may seem only like the inklings of our subconscious that Faith is tested and built.

So then, the problem remains. How can we know what are signs and nudgings and what are not? Fortunately, God does want us to learn and be reassured that he exists despite his invisibility. He wants us to build that faith in him, so often he will reinforce his messages.

This reinforcement can be like for the wedding couple, who got many (more than one, two or three) "coincidental" events or "signs" that together conveyed a common message. Another reinforcement is a very strong nudging, like an idea that you can't get out of your head or a strong urge to speak to someone. He can also reinforce messages with extremely unlikely "coincidental" events. Events so improbable yet they happen.

One example shows how perfect God's timing is and how aware he is of everything going on in the world. When I was on a motorcycle tour of the West in the summer of 2008, my party of four bikes was forced to stop just outside of Rocky Mountain National Park in Colorado. My motorcycle simply went dead and I coasted to a stop on the right side of the road where a small road intersected with the main highway.

Just a few minutes later, as we were trying to figure out why my bike stopped running, someone walked up to us and greeted one of us by name. "Eric!" he said.

We were surprised. Who would know us out here, over a thousand miles from home? It turned out to be Eric's friend who was on vacation. He had a camping spot just up the intersecting road we stopped at. He was just walking back to his camp site when he saw us on the road and recognized Eric.

Now, Eric didn't even know his friend was out there and my bike broke down at exactly the right time and place for us to meet. Mere coincidence? Well, it turned out that Eric's friend was able to help our party continue on, not with my bike but with someone else's.

Another person in our party had brought far too much luggage and it was slowing him so much that we were far behind schedule in the tour. In fact, the wind resistance from the extra luggage was so significant that his bike only made half the miles per gallon it should have. We lost a couple hours when he ran out of gas in the middle of Nebraska the day before and the frequent stops for gas made our progress even slower.

Eric's friend was able to take the extra luggage while we fixed my bike on the spot by hot wiring the ignition. For some reason, the ignition switch had short-circuited and became useless. After that, though, we were able to continue the tour at full speed and arrive at our destination in Lake Tahoe, California just on time for a motorcycle rally that weekend. Were we simply lucky to get this help?

When you look at how improbable this event is, you realize how silly it is that simple luck or chance can explain the perfect timing of my bike's breakdown for our benefit. It is as wishful as giving random variance credit for our existence. There was purpose in this event and seeing that through the context of God makes it much more reasonably probable.

The comforting thing about this example is that it shows He actually does look out for us even when we don't ask for help and even for seemingly unimportant things, such as attending a big motorcycle party. How much more do you think he helps if we did ask and it was for something much more important?

"Surely the arm of the Lord is not too short to save, nor his ear too dull to hear." Isaiah 59:1.

Chains of "signs" or "coincidences" and improbable circumstances are some ways God sends his messages to us. Another way is through a more direct connection to our conscious – dreams. Now here is another medium full of doubt and alternate explanation, but just like with listening to your "gut" God uses the uncertain mechanism of dreams as another way to test and build Faith.

There are many instances in the Bible where God communicates with people through dreams, such as when he told Joseph, the fiancé of Mary, the mother of Jesus, was pregnant through the Holy Spirit and not because she was unfaithful to him. Mary was also told through a dream that she would be the mother to the Son of God. The three wise men or Magi were also instructed not to report back to King Herod about the birth of Jesus through a dream. Even as far back as the times of Genesis, God used dreams. In Genesis 37, he tells Joseph, the son of Jacob (a different person than Mary's Joseph, of course), in dreams that his brothers and in fact, all of Israel would bow down to him.

Like gut feelings, though, dreams can just be dreams and not inspired messages from God. Is there any way to know the difference? Fortunately, there are. The hallmarks of inspired dreams are that they are very vivid. You will remember the dream and its details with ease because when God sends you a message, he does not want it to be forgotten easily like most of our dreams. This vividness also means that the dream will not recur as some of our dreams do, such as the ones born out of stress and anxiety. How many times have you had a dream of falling or being trapped?

Another mark to consider is that during inspired dreams you are much more consciously aware. Some people call this kind of dreaming "lucid" where you are aware that you are dreaming but you are conscious and interacting in the dream as if you were awake in physical reality. However, in lucid dreaming we may take control of the dream and direct it as we wish. God's messages, though, go under his direction so inspired dreams play more like movies that we view.

Sometimes, though, we may interact in these lucid "dreams." Many people, including myself, report coming in contact and interacting with Christ, or an angel of God if not God himself, while in a lucid dream state. We are sleeping yet we are consciously aware and able to communicate, feel, and think during the experience.

My own experiences showed me what his presence feels like and what his voice sounds like. His presence is like a strong energy field – vibrant, vibrating, and rhythmic. His voice sounds like music, also very rhythmic, like trumpet blasts in very quick sequence.

Other people have reported similar experiences around the world and across cultures. These common experiences give a clue that we have built in ways to connect with and perceive the spiritual world and that they are not simply fabrications of a dreaming mind.

The last mark of inspired dreams is that some can be prophetic and tell you that something will happen, so when you think you have had an inspired dream, write down its details and the date you had it. If the events come to pass, you will then have a firm record and reassurance that the dream was inspired, but even if the dream does not turn out to be prophetic, it may still be an important message that you need to take to heart. Writing it down may help you understand it later if it does not make sense at first.

I have often received guidance that I did not understand in the moment but was later shown its meaning through further events. You will be surprised how God can orchestrate his guidance. He has so many avenues of expression that it will simply dumbfound you, so be vigilant and aware of your surroundings in order that you may not miss his clues.

Not everyone will get the same type of guidance either. I mentioned Gifts of the Spirit in Chapter Three and that I am regularly given visions and direct Bible guidance. You may also receive such gifts that help guide you more directly, but don't be discouraged if no extraordinary gifts come to you. God gives these gifts to each of us as he sees fit for the common good.

You may receive gifts, signs, or messages at any time, so just because you have not gotten any now doesn't mean you won't in the future. Also remember that wisdom, knowledge and faith are included in the list of spiritual gifts, and those things are most important for living in Grace successfully.

Building Faith is the most important part of strengthening your relationship with God, so do not continually look for signs or coincidences in your life when they really are not there. True signs will be more obvious and nudge your heart. They will convey a message or purpose. You only need to be more aware of what goes on around you to catch God's signals.

Also, do not constantly test God by asking for proof or for signs. That would be acting against Faith. However, if you are certain of receiving spiritual guidance, and you are unsure of, it is ok to ask for reassurance. Sometimes we have to double-check that the guidance is truly from God and not mere coincidence or from forces that oppose him.

Securing Grace

God said to us, *"Forget the former things; do not dwell in the past. See, I am doing a new thing! Now it springs up; do you not perceive it? I am making a way in the desert and streams in the wasteland."* Isaiah 43:13. His offer of Grace is the *"new thing"* and it is in Grace that God leads us through and out of the wastelands made by our battles with sin. He leads us to walk through the wastelands as he did – absolutely sinless. That is our duty as Christians and *Children of God:*

But you know that [Jesus] appeared so that he might take away our sins. And in him is no sin. No one who lives in him keeps on sinning. No one who continues to sin has either seen him or known him. 1 John 3:5.

Accepting Grace is not a free pass to heaven. We must also strive to be as sinless as possible while we conduct our lives and live in Grace, so forget how you lived your past life and embrace Grace with as much love and passion as Jesus gave when he brought it to us.

The statement in 1 John above does not mean our covenant with God is revoked just because we sin. We will all continue to sin long after we have accepted Grace, whether we know it or not. The critical issue has to do with how we do it or our disposition. It is a matter of the heart.

To understand this, let us break down the terms for fulfilling Grace. Someone has not attained the salvation of Grace until they have fulfilled each condition here and continue to fulfill them up to their moment of death:

1. Believe that Jesus exists now and forever

2. Believe that Jesus is the true Son of God and God Himself

3. Believe that Jesus was here on earth *"in the flesh"*

4. Believe that Jesus was killed on the cross for our sins

5. Believe that Jesus was resurrected in triumph

6. Confess your belief in Jesus to another person, face to face, with personal conviction (not through a "repeat after me" statement)

7. Conduct your life in Grace with a sincere and repentive heart

Failing any condition breaks our agreement with God and revokes our names from the Book of Life. Changing your mind about any statement of belief (1 through 5), denying Jesus before people (6), or conducting sin willfully with insincere and unrepentive intent (7) will all break our promise to God. These all have to do with a change of heart because no one who truly believes in Christ and the New Covenant would willfully break any of these conditions.

It is the condition of your heart, your disposition towards God and what is right, that determines whether you secure your place in heaven. Remember the learning process of mankind in Chapter Five? I said that many of us are not ready for the ideal existence God envisions in heaven, but he offers his help so that we are ready and willing to abide by those ideals.

The reality God created contains the possiblity of good and bad so that free will is possible, and I imagine that in heaven free will is still maintained. After all, the angels also have free will. Therefore, those who secure their place in heaven have free will, but their hearts align with God and his ways. We choose to be righteous. That is the only way that a perfectly good existence can be had in a reality of free will. ALL members of that existence must choose righteousness.

That is why we are tested and filtered through Faith in order to gain entrance into heaven. This is also why it is impossible for man to create a heaven on earth himself. Every person must choose righteousness for the common good, but because of our fallen nature and selfish desires it is impossible for us to achieve without coercion. There will always be people who choose not to follow what is right.

The issue that most confuses people about loosing salvation concerns that of number 7. Some people believe that any act of sin revokes our privilege into heaven unless we sincerely repent of it. This is not quite true, and I did not understand it fully myself until I received guidance that explained it to me.

When we accept Grace, we are given pardon (conditionally as noted above) from all our sins – past, present and future – through the blood of Jesus on the cross. He sacrificed Himself for this purpose. So there is nothing more or less we can do (no works or accomplishments) that will admit us into heaven. We are all simply given pass based on our agreement to Grace.

Those who enter heaven may have committed various degrees of sin, but they are all still in heaven. It is only that some have given way to dishonor while the others are placed in honor. It amounts to the degree of sanctification or purity we have achieved during our life in Grace.

The only people who lose their place in salvation, then, are those who break the conditions of Grace (1 through 7), and breaking Number 7 comes down to committing sin willfully (knowing that God disapproves of the behavior) and without sincere repentance (without remorse for the behavior or the effort to correct oneself in the future). These are matters of the heart, which only God can judge, so do not be disillusioned by anyone who says that you are going to hell for anything you have done.

The real impact of falling to sin has more to do more with our paths in our life maps than with being admitted into heaven. When we keep falling to sin and indulging in wrongful thoughts, speech, or behavior we are actually being led by the paths that sin wants to take us instead of the paths that God wants for us and our overall good.

Persistently sinning in a life of Grace is like being led by a huge, unwashed, and untrained dog on a leash. This is not a helpful, seeing-eye, guide dog, but a disobedient, smelly, mongrel that takes you where *it* wants to go. You do not control it or where you go. That is the danger of following the urges of sin while you live in Grace.

You may never be able to realize the very best that God has intended for you. You want to always follow the true Guide and Compass to reach your overall good in this life, as well as the next. Our accomplishments may not admit us into heaven, but they are counted when God determines our roles in the next life.

Still, it may be hard to understand the difference between sinning with and without sincere repentance. The next section will discuss this further as we try to understand the forces that oppose God's will.

War of Worlds

Now that we have talked about listening to God and his guidance, we can talk about the opposing side's influences on us – how the spiritual war between God's ways and the forces that oppose him affect how we follow (or not follow) God. To understand how this spiritual war affects us, we must acknowledge that the world is under the influence of sin and Satan. In fact, *"the whole world is under the control of the evil one"* 1 John 5:19 and we were *"sold as a slave to sin"* Romans 7:14 as part of our learning process.

We see evidence of this everywhere from all the crimes

committed and all the behavior that goes against God's ideals now and through history. But because sin and Satan have great influence on earth does not mean that God isn't in complete control overall. He gives the dark forces reign where he deems appropriate as a mechanism for teaching and testing us.

Sin and the dark spiritual forces led by Satan work to derail us from God's planned path for us. God himself designed these forces to test our resolve and inclinations, and by working through them and defeating them, we can gain a much greater appreciation for the ideals that he wants us to understand.

It is like the rich child coming into existence with everything he desires at his fingertips. He does not learn appreciation for how good his existence is unless he loses his riches, but the child born to poverty who later earns his riches knows so much better what it is to be rich. He has a basis for comparing both states and can appreciate his good fortune in a way that the other cannot. God teaches us as the poor child. We are born to poverty and slaves to sin, so that in our struggles with sin and hardship, our initial state of weakness makes our strength and victory much more complete in the end.

God says, *"For my power is made perfect in weakness."* 2 Corinthians 12:9. The hardships he gives show us exactly how good the good truly is, for how can we know if we have not seen the bad to measure against? God's method teaches us the true value of what is good and right. It also teaches us virtues that he wants us to hold firm to as we live in Grace: Perseverance, Compassion, Righteousness, and, of course, Faith. So keep on task and stay the righteous course when your personal trials come.

Consider it pure joy, my brothers, whenever you face trials of many kinds, because you know that the testing of your faith

*develops perseverance. Perseverance must finish its work so
that you may be mature and complete, not lacking anything.*
James 1:2

Persevering through the bad parts of our reality builds and tests
Faith – that it is through trust in God that we may overcome all trials
and hardships, come what may. And at the same time, building our
Faith and restoring our spiritual framework allows us to persevere in
later trials with less struggle than before.

It is a cycle that strengthens us in a way that perseverance
without Faith cannot measure to because mere will power can only go
so far before it breaks, and when it does, your entire self breaks with
it. Perseverance in Faith, however, forges and pounds our spirit into
a hardened core that will not buckle under any circumstance. A spirit
forged in Faith is as enduring as God himself because we are assured
by His Word that the faithful are always redeemed in the end.

We know why our world was placed in sin, but what exactly
are these forces opposing God that we must overcome? There are two
main forces. They both work to pull us farther from God's ideals and
from having perfect fellowship with him, but they are very different
from one another. The first is external to us – spiritual entities like
angels except they oppose God. These we call demons, and like God's
influences, theirs are also usually very subtle. They too can nudge our
conscious, give "signs," and drive our desires.

Spirits, both good and bad, have the ability to influence us
by inserting or amplifying thoughts and emotions. The bad ones can
fuel rage, inflame lust, and suggest wrong thoughts and actions. This
may sound silly and unrealistic, like there is a little red devil with a
pitchfork sitting on your shoulder trying to get you to do bad things,
but reality is not far from this cartoonish image. If you accept God and

Jesus as real and true in your life, you must also accept that everything he teaches and says is true. Demons and angels exist and they can have very real influence on us.

This is a scary part of reality, but the good thing is that we have free will and can choose which influences to follow. It is only in very rare cases of demon possession when an individual's behavior can be coerced, but even then the Light of God can defeat the wicked and restore a person to health. All of us, however, have to be able to recognize bad influences to combat them. How then shall we equip ourselves for this spiritual war? With God's defense, of course...

Put on the full armor of God so that you can take your stand against the devil's schemes. For our struggle is not against flesh and blood, but against the powers of this dark world and against the spiritual forces of evil in the heavenly realms.

...

Stand firm then, with the belt of truth buckled around your waist, with the breastplate of righteousness in place, and with your feet fitted with the readiness that comes from the gospel of peace. In addition to all this, take up the shield of faith, with which you can extinguish all the flaming arrows of the evil one. Take the helmet of salvation and the sword of the Spirit, which is the word of God. And pray on all occasions with all kinds of prayers and requests."
Ephesians 6:11

What God wants to convey in this armor metaphor is that the best defense against sin and the dark forces of the world is to do ALL of the following:

- **Belt of Truth** – Hold His Truth firmly as a support
- **Breastplate of Righteousness** – Follow in God's Righteousness (his guidance and ways)
- **Feet fitted with the Gospel of Peace** – Believe in the Gospel of Jesus, that God came *"in the flesh"* as Jesus and offers Grace as an act of mercy and healing
- **Shield of Faith** – Hold Faith in God (believe in him and his promises)
- **Helmet of Salvation** – Believe that Grace is the way to the Kingdom of Heaven
- **Sword of the Spirit** – Use and Know His Word
- **And Pray On All Occasions** – Speak to and ask God for anything and at any time

By using His Armor, constantly polishing it, and having it always ready and fitted while you live in Grace, you will be well protected against the dark forces. Note in the rundown of His Armor, that there is emphasis on knowing and understanding Scripture – trusting, believing, and using it. This is why I said in Chapter Five that His Word is also a standard and measure by which we can discern what is in line with God and what is not, so when you get "signs," nudgings, or other guidance that seems to be of a spiritual nature, use God's standards to test them before acting.

God will never contradict His Word in the Bible so any guidance that opposes His Word or suggests actions that would cause you to sin can be quickly eliminated and rejected. God will also not ask you to follow a path that does not fit your abilities and dispositions. However, he may ask you to follow a difficult and challenging path, like he guided me to quit my job and write this book, as well as to take to the race track.

I knew my abilities were in line with what he wanted me to do, so the guidance was reasonable. But if he told me I should become a professional dancer then the guidance would have been questionable because, honestly, a headless chicken has more coordination than me and likely will run about longer before fainting in front of a crowd.

God's guidance also usually emphasizes helping others in some way, especially to help spread the Truth. Guidance from the dark forces tend to concentrate on selfish desires and gains and quick and easy gratification, as opposed to God's ideals of hard, honest work, discipline, helpfulness, sacrifice, and perseverance.

The subtle nature of spiritual guidance can be very confusing, so it is a good idea to ask in prayer for reassurance and understanding. He may give you wisdom and reinforcement of the guidance in ways that only God could do. Remember that he is omniscient and knows what happens and what you will do before it happens. Satan and demons are limited beings like us. They are not omniscient or omnipotent, so you can judge guidance by God's abilities as well as by His Word.

An example of this kind of guidance reinforcement is when I got the vision of an audience standing in applause (recall my testimony in Chapter Three about quitting my job). Later that day, the vision materialized on the television set. I do not regularly watch television or leave it on, but that day I did.

Only God could know beforehand if I would do this and at what time and on what channel. A skeptic would dismiss such coincidence, but it requires a heart listening with Faith to hear God's messages. However, if you hear a message and are still confused about your guidance, do consult with more experienced people in the Christian community to help you interpret.

Measure everything by God's nature and by His Word. In that way, you can discern his guidance, and in that way there is also *"No*

Other Gospel," as Apostle Paul states in Galatians 1. Nothing that preaches ideas that are contrary the Gospel of Jesus can be from God even if they seemed to have come from an angel of heaven. We can trust God because he never contradicts himself or changes his mind, but Satan uses all sorts of tricks, lies, and deceptions to pull people away from God.

He can disguise the sourness of a lemon with a slick, shiny, and appealing cover, such as using the mask of peace and spiritual fulfillment to countermand belief in Jesus as some gospels preach. What's wrong with peace and spiritual fulfillment without Jesus as God? The problem is that it is an empty fulfillment of the spirit that is not backed up by God. Without belief in our one true God through Jesus, you are turning your back on him and abandoning his hand offered in Grace, which has literal healing power. God's promises are never empty.

He also declared Grace as necessary to rescind our sins and attain fellowship with him in heaven. Every single one of us, no matter how good, peaceful, lawful, moral or enlightened we think we are have sinned in some way or another. We are born slaves into sin. It is inherent in our very nature.

As Apostle Paul says, *"For I have the desire to do what is good, but I cannot carry it out. For what I do is not the good I want to do; no, the evil I do not want to do – this I keep doing. Now if I do what I do not want to do, it is no longer I who do it, but it is sin living in me that does it."* Romans 7:18.

Now, Paul is not making excuses for sinning by blaming it on some kind of alter ego within him, nor is he blaming Satan's influences. He is talking about the second force in our spiritual battles. The first was external, but this one is an internal part of us.

We struggle with wanting to do the right things, but our

biological wiring and pre-programmed instincts for self gratifying behavior often prevent us from doing what is good, or more explicitly, what is right in God's eyes.

This "wiring" can also make our thoughts unclean and put us in sin, so not every bad thought is from spiritual (demonic) influences. However, the dark spiritual forces do use our biological weaknesses and tendencies to further tempt us into sin.

Paul's statement in Romans 7:18 marks the difference between sincere and insincere sinning and repentance, which we talked about in the last section about losing our salvation. If we do not have the desire to do what is good, we also do not have remorse or wish to correct ourselves when we do wrong. That is the kind of heart that will bar you from heaven.

The kind of heart that keeps you in heaven does desire to do good and does want to correct bad behavior, but as Paul states, sometimes the urges of our fallen nature are too strong for us to resist – too strong for mere will power.

The good news, though, is this second force in our spiritual war can be bypassed by working through the filter of Faith. The filter can actually strip off our old instinctual behaviors and give us the complete control of ourselves that we were designed to have.

Gaining that control comes little by little as you live in Faith by following God's ideals, using His Word, and trusting in his promises. Remember, walking in God's paths forges our spirit in a way that mere will power cannot compare to.

The changes are literal and measurable as you find yourself living in fulfillment of God's ideals and taking paths along your life map that would have been impossible without Faith. Skeptics, though, might say the changes are only behavioral – simply a result of following instructions, so why not just get any self-help book?

The first problem with self-help is that it is an approach that relies mainly on personal will power, which is limited and fallible. Self-help is also self centered because it ignores God as a helpful, saving force. It ignores God's far greater wisdom on all matters. And last, there is scientific evidence that God backs up His Word with literal biological change in us through the study of neural brain scan technology.

A speaker at a Christian men's conference who was part of a study of rehabilitated sex addicts found that the healing process of Faith actually rewired his brain to block stimuli, like nudity, from creating unwanted side-effects, such as sexual arousal, that in turn urges us to sin further. Faith and the use of God's Word actually does filter the unwanted parts of our psyche and reprograms our instincts.

Of course, from a scientist's standpoint, this effect can be explained in different ways that have nothing to do with Faith and God. However, recall all the evidence I presented in the first chapters of this book that back up Christianity, much of which can also be explained by other reasons, but when so many unrelated things correlate with one another to support Biblical Truth, the most logical conclusion is that God's Word is true.

Faith actually rewires us to align with God's ideals, but the bad news about our natural sinful state is that it is inescapable that anyone can be entirely free of sin. All of us require the terms of Grace to be forgiven and placed into the right relationship with God.

It does sound one-sided and arrogant of Christianity that Grace is the only way through to salvation. We have been attacked as being intolerant of other viewpoints because of this, but the truth is, Christianity does not teach intolerance. God tells us not to judge people. Only God has that right. The righteous path is to let free will reign and allow people to make their own decisions.

However, we can judge what people say. We can judge other religions, other philosophies, and evidence to figure out what is most reasonable and logical as a whole. *"Preserve sound judgment and discernment, do not let them out of your sight."* Proverbs 3:21. In that way, we had determined Christianity and God's Word to be trustworthy, and we can continue to make discernments using the tools he gave us to follow the correct paths along our life maps.

This is where Bill Wilson's testimony about the UFO experience ties in. This does not seem to make any sense in a discussion of spiritual warfare, but bare with me. I did not understand the connection at first either, but circumstances allowed me to piece together that Skip's UFO was actually a spiritual entity or craft and not an alien spaceship or top secret military airship. The clue to me was that it could not be seen by looking straight at it but only by using peripheral vision.

I had a conversation with someone many months earlier about trying to see ghosts and spirits, and one way is to not look directly at them and use your peripheral vision. The spiritual world is usually hidden from us, but something about our peripheral vision can sense things in that realm. This is why we sometimes see fleeting movement of people or shapes in our peripheral vision, but when we turn to look there is nothing there.

God's guidance here is that he made Skip witness to this UFO for a reason, and he offers an explanation that fits this chapter. The UFO phenomena are actually a test of Faith for mankind because there will come a time when we are given statements by apparently "out of this world" beings that are contrary to God's Word, and we will be faced with believing it or not. When those times come, remember this discussion, remember the full armor of God, and *preserve sound judgment and discernment.*

Wielding the Sword of the Spirit – His Word

One of the reason's God gave us His Word was to equip us through life, to defend ourselves and win in the battles with sin. It is the Sword of His Spirit, which is a part of the Armor of God mentioned above. The last section stated why it is important to know and understand God's Word and that reading the Bible and going to church are good ways to learn.

I also stated that trust in His Word is also important because like a physical weapon or tool, you cannot use it with full effect if you do not trust it. In the same way, you must fully trust God's Word as perfect and true to make it most effective. He gave it to us from his superior wisdom so that we could use it to improve and understand our lives. I could not have framed the Big Picture or come to understand our reality if I did not trust His Word, so you too must trust it completely.

You opened the window when you accepted Grace, but you must also bind the curtains up to let the Light penetrate the hollows of your heart and allow your inside – your spirit – to receive its full impact. In this way, opening the curtains and trusting in the power of His Word has the ability, quite literally, to change and renew your entire self, both inner (spiritual) and outer (physical).

No man-made mechanisms – not self-help, will power, medication, surgery, nor institutions – have the power to change our spiritual selves and at the same time our physical selves in the way that God can. His Word has literal power behind it because God backs it up with actual, literal change. Consider what Jesus says here:

No one sews a patch of unshrunk cloth on an old garment. If he does, the new piece will pull away from the old, making the tear worse. And no one pours new wine into old wineskins. If he does, the wine will burst the skins, and both the wine and the wineskins will be ruined. No, he pours new wine into new wineskins. Mark 2:21

A common interpretation of this passage is that Jesus brings a new way of thinking and doing things in which old ways must be thrown out. This is certainly true. Remember, *"Forget the former things..."* earlier? However, there is another message conveyed in this metaphor – that when our spiritual renewal comes, the restored spiritual self comes with a complete restored self.

In other words, when Faith renews our spiritual side the rest of us follows, so no matter your physical condition – ill, failing, broken, or destitute – you can be restored if your spirit is strengthened. On the other hand, if your spiritual side is weak then no amount of physical health or material prosperity can heal your spiritual side. Having a strong spiritual framework can get you through any physical or emotional adversity, but a weak spirit will allow your physical self to collapse when difficult times come.

God designed us and knows the best way to change and improve us, so trust Him to do it by trusting and understanding His Word. Open the window and let the Light in. That is necessary to wield the Sword correctly, but another thing you must do to master any tool is to practice with it. In that way, to get the full benefit of His Word you must also use it regularly. To do this, consider the first part of Psalm 1, which I introduced at the end of Chapter Three:

Blessed is the man
who does not walk in the counsel of the wicked
or stand in the way of sinners
or sit in the seat of mockers.

But his delight is in the law of the Lord
and on his law he meditates day and night.
He is like a tree planted by streams of water,
which yields its fruit in season
and whose leaf does not wither.
Whatever he does prospers.
Psalm 1:1

Note the second verse, *"But his delight is in the law of the Lord and on his law he meditates day and night."* Take that statement, not literally, but to heart. It says to love and trust God's Word (have faith in it) and think about it constantly, so not only do you open the window and bind the curtains up, but you must also sit in front of the window, face it and look out at the light as much as possible in order that you may receive its full benefit.

Meditate here is not the same as the meditate we often think of when we envision a bald monk sitting and chanting all day, every day. Not everyone has the determination, focus, or time to do that type of meditation, and honestly, that is not the kind of life God wants for us. He wants us to live life, not bind ourselves to a mat and ponder endlessly within ourselves.

However, we have a spiritual side and intense meditation can give greater access to that part of us by putting our minds into a state akin to REM sleep, but it is also very important to acknowledge that God is external to us as well as a part of us. So do not concentrate inwardly on your own self and make your own reality as many meditative practices teach. That may relax your body and focus your mind, but it does not put you in fellowship with God.

He wants us to be in true fellowship with Him, and the only way to do that is to look outward, directly at God himself, and treat him as real and personal to you. We do that by acknowledging him through Jesus and speaking to him just as with a regular person by your side.

The meditate part of this means to contemplate His Word *"day and night,"* not just in prayer but all the time, constantly, as you go about life – keep His Word on the forefront of your mind and close to your heart. Don't just read or recite it, but think about its meaning.

Use it as you conduct your life to understand and evaluate, not only your actions, but your thoughts as well. His Word is your guard for blocking the attacks of sin and unrighteousness in the spiritual war. It will keep you protected from losing your way along your life map, so be fully aware of all your thoughts and actions, and make them compliant to God's will.

For though we live in the world, we do not wage war as the world does. The weapons we fight with are not the weapons of the world. On the contrary, they have divine power to demolish strongholds. We demolish arguments and every pretension that sets itself up against the knowledge of God, and we take captive every thought to make it obedient to Christ.
2 Corinthians 10:3

Make *"captive every thought to make it obedient to Christ"* by holding them up to God's Word and then rejecting them if they do not comply or align with His ways. Then replace those thoughts and behavior with ones that do align with God. This is how we renew ourselves and *"demolish strongholds."*

The strongholds are the fortresses the dark spiritual forces set up in our minds and attack us with. They are the negative thoughts and emotions (either internal or external in origin) that try to bind us to failure, confusion, depression, and sin. God gave us the Sword of His Spirit so that we could be conquerors in Christ, but it takes discipline and complete awareness of yourself (your thoughts and actions) to wield His Sword correctly.

We will talk about discipline later. More important in this discussion is to find what part of His Word to use? How do we know what Scripture out of the thousand pages to use in our personal spiritual battles?

You can find Scripture for a certain subject by using the topical index at the end of your Bible or during reading the Bible or listening to sermons make note of any Scripture that stands out for you in the moment. Many Christian resources provide devotionals too, which are Scripture passages and prayers for certain occasions or purposes.

Finding Scripture that is best for you should be easy. God generally works subtly through the Holy Spirit (your constant connection to Him with your own spirit) by nudging your conscience and highlighting certain thoughts and stimuli for you. Try to listen with your "gut" as we talked about in the section titled "Listening to God."

Once you have found Scripture that speaks to you personally, keep it on hand, or better yet, memorize it so that it is close to you and in your heart. Then when the situation calls for your heart to be calmed or a temptation to be squelched, take out His Word, remind yourself of what it means, and follow its wisdom.

Keep your Light lit. Have His Word constantly "on" while you go about business. Recite His Word during your mind's idle time. It is the best way to stoke the brilliance of God's wisdom in your heart.

Furthermore, during prayer ask for wisdom so you may understand better the things that God wants you to understand. You will be surprised how much insight the Holy Spirit can give you. It can be leaps and bounds beyond what you can think up on your own.

Much of the content of the Bible comes from this kind of inspired wisdom, which is why it is deemed as God's Word even though it took human hands to record it.

Demonstrate Desire

"The path of the righteous is like the first gleam of dawn, shining ever brighter till the full light of day." Proverbs 4:18

You saw that *"first gleam of dawn"* when you first accepted Grace, and you will see it turn to full light as you continue on in Faith, but you must sit in front of the window often and spend your time in God's Light. This means being in fellowship with him as often as possible – through daily prayer, through regular worship, through studying the Bible, through being obedient in his ways, through belief in his promises, and through thinking of him and giving him your thoughts at any time for any reason or matter whatsoever. This is the kind of fellowship he wants from us – a true, trusting and loving fellowship of father to child and friend to friend.

Living in a true fellowship with God frees us from the ritualized life that most people think of when they think of being religious. If he wanted us to emphasize rituals he would have spelled them out for us just as he did for the Israelites in the Old Testament. Instead, God made a new agreement with us in Grace and now he only asks that we sincerely be in fellowship with him through Jesus.

Therefore do not let anyone judge you by what you eat or drink, or with regard to a religious festival, a New Moon celebration or a Sabbath day. These are a shadow of the things that were to come; the reality, however is found in Christ. Colossians 2:16.

There are few exceptions to the ritual rule, so it is not important that we celebrate one holiday or another, nor will God condemn us if we skip going to church sometimes or if we choose not to participate in a religious fast or demonstration. Living in fellowship with God negates the need for ritual. However, as in our earthly relationships with one another, any aspect of showing your devotion and love for someone is noticed, wanted, and appreciated.

That is why you should worship God at church regularly and take part in holidays that celebrate what he has done. Do it out of desire to maintain that relationship, not to satisfy man-made rituals or to look good in the eyes of others. Public displays of godly devotion are always good so long as they are not overtly public in an effort to make you appear holier or "better" than others. We are all equal in the Body of Christ. All of us will be crowned with his glory and inherit his kingdom.

In fellowship will your Faith mature, and by demonstrating your desire – your Faith – in all these ways are expressions of the First Commandment, *"Love the Lord."* All of it and anything else you do to express that desire for God further builds Faith, so in that way Faith is the most perfect and complete form of realizing the First Commandment.

As you keep moving forward in Faith and letting God guide and help you, allow your fellowship with him to bloom into that perfect expression of the First Commandment. Allow yourself to love God as he loves you. Return His Grace with your appreciation and devotion because that is really all he wants from us. What else can we give to someone who created and owns everything? Our hearts and souls and very selves.

Demonstrate desire. Don't just pray and speak to him. Sing to him with all your heart, mind, and soul. The harmony of fellowship rings most true by way of music and joy because it mirrors the melodies of heaven. Music and song are some of the most tangible forms of love there could be. We can feel beat and melody as their vibrations resonate through us. Poetic lyrics, too, evoke emotion and when combined with music, their effect resonates so strongly with the themes of heaven that God can't help but smile when we sing to him. Do your best, then, to sing those songs in church and whenever else you can.

Most rituals are optional, but there are some things that God wants us to do when we have accepted Grace. One is to participate in communion to remember his sacrificial act of body and blood, and the other is to be water baptized. Jesus made it a point to be baptized himself by John the Baptist even though John insisted that Jesus baptize him instead. *Jesus replied, "Let it be so now; it is proper for us to do this to fulfill all righteousness." then John consented.* Matthew 3:15.

I had even been given guidance very early in my journey in Grace to be water baptized. It was a step in Faith that I did not think much of doing because of my introverted nature, but God made it a point for me to do it, so I believe it is a very important display of devotion that symbolically parallels Jesus' example of dying on the cross and subsequent resurrection.

To emphasize this further, Jesus says in Matthew 28:18, *"All authority in heaven and on earth has been given to me. Therefore go and make disciples of all nations, baptizing them in the name of the Father and of the Son and of the Holy Spirit, and teaching them to obey everything I have commanded you. And surely I am with you always, to the very end of the age."*

God commands baptism as a specific duty to go along with the other duties of that passage, titled *"The Great Commission."* This commission tells us to share the Truth to the rest of the world. As much as some of us would like to stay at home and keep to ourselves, God created mankind to be a Body that works together, so to be good Christians we must go out and interact with one another to share in the joy of fellowship with God, help each other, and spread the Gospel.

This does not mean we need to be persistent evangelists or preachers of the Word everywhere we go. Being a missionary is not for everyone. God simply wants us to be a light for others to follow, an example, just as Jesus was. This means showing God's ideals in how you interact with others – being forgiving, helpful, merciful, and righteous. The First Commandment is meant to instruct us in fellowship with God, but the Second Commandment is for our fellowship with one another.

Love your neighbor, even your enemy, as yourself. Loving each other is not the romantic sense of love, but the brotherly or sisterly form of it – understanding each other and having compassion. Remember that we are all more alike than different, and all of us have fallen to sin.

However, if you have opportunities to minister to people in need, then do it as God does it – with grace and respect. He is not in our face with his offer and so we should not be in each others' when we shine our lights. Help people by suggesting they attend church with you, suggest Christian help groups or resources, or simply talk to them and consul them with your Godly experiences and knowledge.

Be a light for Christ wherever you go and in all you do. Represent Him righteously. He clothed us in Grace so that its effects can be seen. Your Faith is not meant to be a club over someone's head, but it is not meant to be hidden either – *"No one lights a lamp and hides it in a jar or puts it under a bed. Instead, he puts it on a stand, so that those who come in can see the light."* Luke 8:16.

God needs us to shine and do his work on earth because of his subtle ways, so do not cower in a corner or be *"ashamed of the gospel, because it is the power of God for the salvation of everyone who believes."* Romans 1:16.

Body of Sharing

God needs us to do his work, but spreading the Gospel is not our only duty as faithful Christians. We must also help enable the Body of Christ to do whatever work is needed, and in our society that enablement is most often financial because goods, materials, and services need to be paid for

The subject of tithing and giving to the church is probably the least favorite subject for everyone, but it must be discussed in a complete view of God's ideals. He designed mankind to work as one Body, so just as some parts of our bodies may become weak or injured, some of us may also be in need of support and help at times.

God could certainly rain down gold and jewels on the needy or heal all injuries and illness if he wanted to, but his ways are subtle and he wants us to learn the reasons for his ideals. Instant gratification does not teach us anything other than to expect more instant gratification.

Instead, he wants us to work together and with Him for the common good, so he needs us to step forward and share in our better fortunes so that the less fortunate can be cared for. You may not think you can afford to give regularly to church and charity, but consider that the average, middle-class American income is ranked in the upper three percent of incomes worldwide and that the richest one percent of the world receive as much or more than the bottom half of the world. What exactly are we spending all that money on when the majority of the world is living in poverty and need?

Also consider that God actually owns everything. He is Creator and King, and ultimately, is responsible for all our fortunes. In that way, we do not truly own anything – not our possessions or money. We are merely stewards or managers of what God gives us, and it is his wish that we manage our resources righteously, so that the entire Body he created can be blessed with our good will.

Our blessings of charity, no matter how big or small, bless us in return because God favors the righteous. Our charity can also affect the needy in ways and in places we could never reach on our own or even imagine. Not only can the poor be feed and clothed, but lives can be saved in this life and the next, because often the people who receive support will see the light of Grace in it and come to accept Grace as well. How can you put a price on that?

However, we must put a price on it so that we know how much to give. A common rule that has Biblical support is ten percent of your income. In fact, a tithe means a tenth. But that is only a guideline because the tenth was originally mandated to the Jews in the Old Testament to help support the priesthood and seasonal festivals. In the New Testament there is no mention of specific amounts to give to the church with one exception. Jesus did ask his disciples for **everything** when they followed him – mind, body, and possessions. He instructed them to sell everything so that the money could be shared among everyone. The apostles continued this practice in the church after Jesus was glorified on the cross as well.

Now, of course, God is not telling us to do the same thing today. The situation for the disciples was different and Jesus meant to test them by asking for everything. However, God still tests us today as well. Consider your financial contributions to tithing (your church) and other charities a test of Faith because it takes faith to give that money and trust that it is used for God's purposes.

Some of us have become cynical because of the many scandals about religious and charity leaders misusing the money given to them, but also know that God always sees that justice is served in the end. Just use your best judgment when you give and make the tenth guideline. You may give more or less based on your means and level of generosity. It is not so much the amount that is given but the act that matters. It is another act of Faith that demonstrates your desire and fellowship with God.

For if the willingness is there, the gift is acceptable according to what one has, not according to what he does not have. Our desire is not that others might be relieved while you are hard pressed, but that there might be equality.
2 Corinthians 8:12

Whoever sows sparingly will also reap sparingly, and whoever sows generously will also reap generously. Each man should give what he has decided in his heart to give, not reluctantly or under compulsion, for God loves a cheerful giver. And God is able to make all grace abound in you, so that in all things at all times, having all that you need, you will abound in every good work. 2 Corinthians 9:6.

This service that you perform is not only supplying the needs of God's people but is also overflowing in many expressions of thanks to God. Because of the service by which you have proved yourselves, men will praise God for the obedience that accompanies your confession of the gospel of Christ, and for your generosity in sharing with them and everyone else. 2 Corinthians 9:12

Tests of Faith

We just mentioned that giving financially to the church is a test of Faith. There are many more tests, because as we continue along in our relationship with God, filtering through life with Faith, our devotion will wax and wane as we settle into a Christian lifestyle.

Everyone will come across things that take our attention away from God, such as having children, getting married, moving, or changing careers. The fervor and passion of our first days in Grace may become subdued, so we must see to it that we maintain our fellowship with God.

Most of us during the first few months of stepping through Faith will become accustomed to praying and giving God our thoughts daily no matter what circumstances we are in, but when life calls we often do not have time to read, study or meditate on His Word or worship him as much as we did when we started. Some days we may forget to pray and be in fellowship entirely as we jump straight out of bed, rush to our meetings, and fall straight to sleep after a long day.

Fortunately, God will not protest if life takes us away for a time. He understands us completely and does want us to live life to its fullest. He will be patient and simply wait for us, expecting us to come back to the open window, always ready to return our wave with a bright smile. So live your life, but don't let its struggles and obligations take you too far from the window. You always want His Light in sight.

The hum and buzz of our swift, modern lives can be very distracting, but remember, anything that takes us away from perfect fellowship with God is sin, so to help maintain fellowship, understand the line between passion and obsession. Passion is good. God wants us to have passion in all things we do and put forth our best efforts. We control passion, but obsession spills into sin because it starts to control our behavior. This takes away from our fellowship with God because he wants us in complete control of ourselves.

When we are obsessed over something, we constantly think about it and keep coming back to activities that satisfy those thoughts. We make judgments and choices that help satisfy the obsession instead of giving all options their deserved weight.

Furthermore, satisfying obsession can become uncontrollable and when that happens it becomes addiction, which can force you onto destructive life paths and requires a lot more effort to steer yourself back onto the path God intends for you.

There are so many things in our commercialized society today that are designed to take and keep our attention and spawn obsession in an effort to maximize profits. Television, video games, toys, gambling, sports, instant communications, and Internet web sites are just a sampling, but anything can become an obsession. Being fully aware of our thoughts and actions as well as what goes on around us is another aspect of listening to God, so use your listening abilities to block obsession as well as other sin. Meditate on it *day and night* as we discussed before about wielding His Word.

Check your thoughts and actions in order that you can recognize sin, including obsession, and squelch them before they become a problem. If you find yourself making certain activities more important than they need to be then remind yourself of God's example in Jesus. He was absolutely disciplined, and we must strive to be the same.

Relax your surging heart and take a step back from satisfying obsessive thoughts. Reject them. Prioritize your duties appropriately and make God priority one, because when you place him and his ideals foremost in mind, everything else will fall in line and discipline will naturally settle in.

Putting God first in your life does not mean you should neglect everything else or make it an excuse to put other things off. It means filtering and checking every thought and action against His ideals. It also means using prayer, not as routine duty but as acts of fellowship, so pray often and whenever you have a need to speak to Him, such as when you are stressed or feel sinful urges hard to resist. Just stop whatever you are doing and take a break for prayer.

All you need to do is find a quiet place and pray for help, resilience, wisdom or whatever else you may need. It can only take a few minutes, but the effect of prayer is that it strengthens God's Spirit in us, which will help us receive his guidance and calm our own spirits so that we may be disciplined.

Discipline is self-control. It is another virtue that brings us closer to fellowship with God, so anything that takes from our abilities to control ourselves then becomes sin. This is why obsession, addiction, drunkenness and substance or drug abuse is sin. These things subdue our self-control and disarms the alarms of our conscience so that the door is left wide open for our pre-programmed instincts to take control. Once our guard is down, those sinful nudges can then easily lead us down paths of much worse sins, such as lust into rape and anger into rage.

Be vigilant, aware and listening of your thoughts and behavior to keep that guard posted in your conscience. Don't submit to activities that take down your guard. You don't want to become a puppet to your animal instincts nor to the dark spiritual forces. Now, this does not mean you cannot drink alcohol at all. It means knowing the appropriate limit and stopping when you've reached it.

One drink is safe for most everyone, but after that, monitor and discipline yourself. Everyone is different, so I cannot recommend an absolute limit, but most likely, once you notice the numbing of your senses and boost of pleasure (that "buzz") then you've hit your limit.

Living life is not the only thing that may make our Faith bob up and down. God also tests our faith by giving us trials and asking for perseverance. Sometimes we doubt God and our Faith fades a notch when he does not seem to answer our prayers or when things don't happen as we want or expect.

Remember though, that God hears all our prayers, but he does things for our overall good as well as for The Overall Good in ways that we could never imagine. He may decide that going through a hardship and learning discipline is better for you than to pluck you out of a tough experience, never to understand the true value of his ideals.

God doesn't test us for his benefit or to measure us because he already knows exactly what we do before we do it. The trials he gives us are for our benefit. Remember that we are in a learning process. We are being filtered and taught by Faith and are actually being changed by that process. He wants us to be complete and mature beings with a full understanding of reality.

This is why God allowed Job to be tested in the Book of Job. He allowed Satan to torment Job and take away almost everything he had, even though God knew he was a faithful and righteous person. Job lost his family, riches, health, and respect, and thought God had turned against him. He blamed God for all his hardship, but still through it all, he held on to Faith and believed in God. He said, *"I know that my Redeemer lives, and that in the end he will stand upon the earth. And after my skin has been destroyed, yet in my flesh I will see God; I myself will see him with my own eyes – I and not another. How my heart yearns within me!"* Job 19:25.

Job's love for the Lord never faltered, though he was tested harshly. He was innocent of wrongdoing but like the rest of us, God wanted him to learn the full measure of what is good. In that way, I believe God tests all of us in our Faith, though most of us will not be given as difficult a time as Job.

When hardships come, though, remember Job's solid Faith, but try not to blame God as he did. Instead, set your downcast eyes forward to see through difficulties and suffering. Keep trust in God's wisdom and justice, though you may not understand it, and be reassured that God always has you understand in the end.

However, if your Faith does falter and you turn your back to God, remember your agreement in Grace. He will forgive you for doubting and turning away. You only need to come back to him and try better next time. This leads me into further personal testimony to illustrate how God tests and teaches us because some of the reasons God told me to take to the race track was to test my Faith and teach me perseverance.

On November 24th, 2008, I had a vivid dream where I was riding a race bike as fast as I could but there was a strong wind against me. It was so strong that it slowed my bike, and when I tried to shift into a lower gear and go faster to compensate, the wind blew against me stronger so that I could not make progress. Now, I had already gotten guidance that racing was to be a part of my future and I continued to get that guidance long after this dream, but the dream contradicted that guidance. Was it just a dream from my anxieties, or was there a different message?

On Saturday, April 25th, 2009, I took to the race track for the first time to wean myself into the environment with some track days. Track days are not racing but more like practice sessions. It was intimidating, and I was nervous about it even though I had over a decade of fast sport riding experience on the street. And to further my anxieties, I ran into some "bad luck."

We had just arrived at the track and were setting up our bikes and gear under a canopy shelter. When we were just walking back with another load of equipment, we found my bike had fallen over off its stand. It could have been the wind, but that was unusual, and it did not make me feel confident when I was already apprehensive. Fortunately, the only damage done were a few scratches to the paint.

The weather too contributed to my mood. It was very poor, cold and rained much of the time. I thought that when God sent you on a mission, everything would go well and easy. The sun would always shine and victories would be handed over with no effort, but this weekend felt completely the opposite.

I became even more discouraged after the first couple of sessions on track. Riding the race track at high speed was much more different and difficult than I imagined. I found my street riding experience did not translate well into the race environment. I would need to learn many more skills, and I started to think and question God, "Why am I even here? Why do you send me here, Lord, when, clearly, I am not going to win any races anytime soon?"

I kept on riding, though, and after lunch I started getting more comfortable on the track, but then the rain started coming down hard, and we stopped. We checked the forecast for the rest of the day and Sunday and they were full of heavy rain, near 100% chance of precipitation, so we decided to call the weekend a wash and leave early.

On the way home, I kept thinking that racing doesn't seem to be working out. There seemed to be too many things going against me. The money needed for it was significant, the time commitment was large as well, my skills were insufficient, even the weather seemed to conspire against me. Maybe that dream I had did mean I shouldn't do it, and so I doubted all the other guidance I got.

However, coming back early allowed me to go to church

service on Sunday, and the funny thing is, the sermon was about doubting God and jumping in faith. The pastor talked about how Apostle Peter denied Jesus three times after Jesus was captured. Jesus had told Peter this would happen, but he doubted it.

"I tell you the truth," Jesus answered, *"this very night, before the rooster crows, you will disown me three times."* Matthew 26:34.

The pastor continued to say that after Jesus died and was resurrected, he appeared to the disciples while they were fishing in a boat, and out of love for the Lord, Peter leapt into the water to reach Jesus on shore.

This image immediately brought to mind a vision I had on March 4th, 2009 of a red bird swimming in water. It had clambered onto a floating platform, quickly dried, and took off flying. Then the bird was superimposed with a speeding race bike. At the time, I interpreted the vision to mean that my path in racing would lift me out of the mire of life and sin, and so I should keep on that path.

Now though, I understood that I was the red bird and like Peter I should jump into the water in full Faith. I was supposed to come home early from the race track that weekend and go to service to hear His message at exactly the right time. I realized all the difficulties I had were there to test me, to test my Faith, and so I felt bad that I doubted God.

The next day during prayer, my Bible opened directly to John 21:15, exactly in the section titled *"Jesus Reinstates Peter"* where Peter is forgiven his doubt and denial, and in that way, the Lord forgave me as well.

It is now the end of September, and I have since gotten my racing license and completed a season of racing, but it has been a very difficult time. The dream I had last November turned out to be a prophetic message saying I would have many difficulties on this path.

I have had three bad crashes on the track and often considered quitting, but just before my crash in August my direct Bible guidance was James 1, which I quoted earlier when I discussed perseverance. *"...the testing of your faith develops perseverance. Perseverance must finish its work so that you may be mature and complete, not lacking in anything."* James 1:3.

In addition to perseverance, the Lord also uses this path in racing to teach me his principles concerning discipline (keeping self-control under stress) and humility. On the last weekend of racing, I blew the start for the first race because I forgot to put the bike in gear. Dozens of bikes roared around me as they launched while I was frustratingly trying to put the bike into gear. Once, twice, three times it would not click into gear. Finally, the gearbox clunked and I was the last one off the line.

I quickly caught up to the main group as I pushed myself harder and faster than I had ever gone before. I made my fastest lap times during this race, however, in my zeal to catch up I lost focus and crashed hard in a corner with only a quarter of a lap to go before finishing. I did not crash because I was going too fast for my abilities or for the bike's capabilities. I crashed because I made a mistake.

The discipline that I had been practicing on the track was gone when the rush of rage overwhelmed my focus and self-control. In the rage of fumbling the start so badly and of being so far behind, the animal instinct to simply battle took control of my higher thinking and I forgot to lean the bike properly to maintain traction. My tires slid out from under me and I went tumbling off the track into a cloud of dust.

This experience parallels the results of many of our battles with sin. When we are caught up in the heat of a moment we can quickly loose our self-control and make mistakes that put us further into sin and farther away from fellowship with God. This is why discipline is so important in our battles. Take it very seriously. Do not be complacent about listening and monitoring yourself.

After the crash, I was disappointed, but I was still in good spirits to continue racing the next day. I thought I could do very well because my lap times were quick enough to place me with the top finishers.

The next day, though, I came in dead last every single time, one race, after another, after another (four in all). I was very disappointed to end the season like that and also surprised, because I knew I was much faster than that. In one of the races, I had even lost five positions right in the last moments. I couldn't believe it. The wind did indeed seem to be blowing against me.

At the end of the day while in poor spirits, I asked the Lord for guidance and my Bible opened to the pages of Matthew 19:13 to 21:15, where there are no less than three stories concerning humility. They all end with the same theme:

But many who are first will be last, and many who are last will be first. Matthew 19:30

So the last will be first, and the first will be last. Matthew 20:16

Instead, whoever wants to become great among you must be your servant, and whoever wants to be first must be your slave – just as the Son of Man did not come to be served, but to serve, and to give his life as a ransom for many. Matthew 20:26

God was reminding me how important it is to maintain discipline and humility, least we succumb to the perils of our mistakes and Pride. Once more, He humbled me with his very poignant teaching. There is no place for Pride and arrogance in the kingdom of heaven, and those who seek to be first will be last. I smiled as I realized his message, but I did ask him, "Did you have to literally make me come in last to make your point?"

I do not know where racing will lead me, but if I was just sent on that path to be complete in Faith and understanding so that I could convey God's teaching to you here, that is okay with me. The experience has been as exhilarating as it has been difficult. I wouldn't trade his wisdom and methods for anything. I do hope that you too will come to the same conclusion in your own journey through Faith.

Perfect Circle

We began this chapter with a summation of the previous: Love is the motivation, Faith the means, and Fellowship the reward. This statement summarizes the "Why?" of our reality, but as is often with God, he does not stop there. He loves everything to be perfectly elegant and in harmony, so you should not be surprised that very same statement also summarizes this chapter and how he wants us to follow him.

Love is the motivation, Faith the means, and Fellowship the reward.

Make love your motivation to look up to your God, Jesus Christ. Make Faith your means to express that love, and let it work in you to give his promised healing from sin. Then in doing so, your reward is Fellowship with Him in **this** life, as well as the next.

In this life, Fellowship means he will be your Compass, your Guide, and Friend. It means trusting Him completely to guide you in ways and to destinations you could never have imagined. He will lift your burdens from you in the infinite strength he provides, and while he does all that, he will also teach and help you go through that filter of Faith, so you are ready to live that promised eternal life with him in the ideal kingdom he designed for us from the beginning. God wants us to complete that perfect circle with Him. All you need to do is accept his hand in Grace, follow on in Faith, and return His Love with yours.

Prophecies and the Last Days

God wants us to go full circle with him, the entire 360 degrees from the time we first accepted him in Grace until he fulfills his promise of returning to us here on earth once more – the second coming of Christ. We're not quite there yet, but our journey is getting ever closer with each passing tick of the clock, and now even in this moment he has given us signs in his subtle ways that say, "The time is near."

Something I have come to understand during my journey into Faith is that we are in the Biblical Age of the Last Days. Remember in my personal testimony that I was guided to the following Scripture on January 30th, 2009 to help me explain and debate my position on Christianity:

In the last days, God says, I will pour out my Spirit on all
people. Your sons and daughters will prophesy, your young
men and women will see visions, your old men will dream
dreams. Even on my servants, both men and women,
I will pour out my Spirit in those days, and they will prophesy.
I will show wonders in the heaven above and signs on the earth
below, blood and fire and bellows of smoke.
The sun will be turned to darkness and the moon to blood
before the coming of the great and glorious day of the Lord.
And everyone who calls on the name of the Lord will be saved.
Acts 2:17

This passage notes the reason for the visions I was given before I came to accept Grace (the clock of sunlight and the fox and monkey). It also notes that God will pour his Spirit on all people – sons and daughters, men and women, young and old – at this time, so I am far from alone in experiencing supernatural things. There is personal testimony everywhere today if one cares to look and see with completely open eyes.

The passage also notes further signs to recognize the Last Days – *wonders in the heaven above and signs on the earth below.* There are two, literally, shining examples of the signs in heaven that have triggered nudgings in me since I have been led in Faith, but there may be more that I have missed, and there will likely be more to come.

The first I noted was a very rare grouping of the moon with two bright stars (actually planets) in early December 2008. It shows the crescent moon with these stars in a way that inspired my notion of the 3rd Compass (see the cover art of this book for a depiction of the moon and stars).

The second heavenly sign came months later in the spring of 2009 from a photo taken by NASA's Chandra X-ray observatory (below). It shows an apparently ghostly human hand reaching out at a glowing mass in the distance.

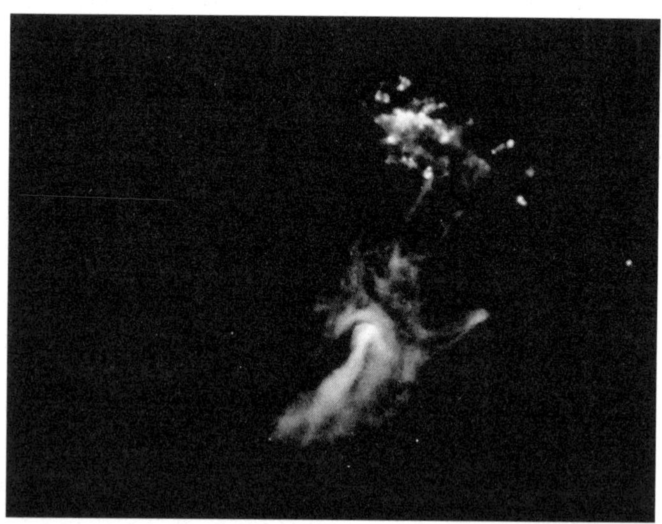

Hand of God?
(see Insert 4 for color photo; courtesy NASA)

Technically, the hand is formed from the energy of a rapidly rotating pulsar (a collapsed star, which is the bright spot in the wrist of the hand) and the glowing orange mass in the background is an energized cloud of gas or star cluster.

Astronomical phenomenon can form many interesting shapes, such as the well known horse head or Pegasus nebula that resembles a horse's head. But the remarkable thing about this hand is the timing of its appearance, and second, the exact anatomical correctness of the hand.

From an artist's viewpoint, the hand shows perfectly a right hand reaching out (and in correct three-dimensional perspective) at an object in the background. This stellar portrait is much more complex and accurate in detail than all the myriad other nebula or galaxy images that have only a passing resemblance to other things, like a horse head, crab, hat, or bow tie.

Last and most important, the hand portrait conveys a Biblical message. Symbolically, the hand is reaching out for something. From my guidance, it has been made clear to me that God's kingdom, the kingdom of heaven, is represented by a great, glowing treasure, jewel, or orb. Furthermore, the hand is a right hand, in which there are references in the Bible to God's Righteous Right Hand.

What I see here is that God is nudging us with this sign to reach out for his kingdom of heaven, which in this case also turns out to literally be in "heaven." **Reach out for the kingdom of heaven is His message**, and He does it in such an elegant and poetic way that only those who have Faith can truly appreciate its eloquence.

The signs in heaven are intriguing but still subtle. The signs on the earth below are even more so: *Blood and fire and bellows of smoke.* These refer to things that have been increasing more and more in recent years around the world, and are still coming to a peak.

Widespread bloodshed from wars and atrocities is apparent around the world and death from famine, disease, and natural disasters is increasing. Fire and smoke from massive wild fires are spread across America and abroad. Increasing volcanic and tectonic activity also contribute to these earthly signs.

The H1N1 flu pandemic is even part of the *signs on the earth* as I have received guidance related specifically to this disease. The details of these revelations as well as others concerning the Last Days are discussed more fully in the free supplement to this book: *Messages from the 3rd Compass*. It is available free in digital form at the web site, 3rdCompass.com.

All of these signs show God's subtle nature and so can easily be dismissed by those without Faith. They call these signs as nothing more than cycles in our earth's history and mere cosmic variances and everyday occurrences. The combined message of all this, though, is that the purpose of all the signs and events of the Last Days are a concentrated effort to get mankind to recognize God's Truth and accept Grace in order that we may reach for that glowing treasure in heaven.

God has been quite subtle. However, I have received guidance that there will be a time when He replaces subtlety with a sledgehammer. Even so, the Last Days should not be feared. They are not about the end of our existence, our world, or anything like that. We will continue on. These are the last days that he withholds the heavy hammer and stays his strength. These are the last days we are given to accept his hand offered in Grace. They only mark a shift in God's learning process for mankind.

Remember the Big Picture in Chapter Five and the Learning Process I spoke of. Mankind has been given the last two thousand years since Jesus came so that we could mature further and accept God's offer of Grace. That was ample time for His Gospel to reach all the ends of the earth and for us to progress technologically and scientifically so that we could understand more completely how God relates to us and our reality.

Before the computer age, advanced mathematics, and the notion of simulations, the concepts of God being outside and also inside our reality, as I explained in Chapter Five, was very difficult if not impossible to convey.

The Last Days mark an end to the study period and pop quizzes. God has been testing us all along, but now we are in the final exam when the faith of mankind is tested most completely. We are being sifted with more vigor through the filter of Faith. Yet, the testing so far have been designed with subtlety. So subtle that many of us overlook it completely. It is as subtle as a breeze that blows the chaff from the wheat as they are repeatedly thrown in the air. Little by little, though, with each bounce, Faith remains solid while Sin blows away.

The exam is a long one, though, (no one knows how long the Last Days will last for certain), so if you've missed some questions, don't worry about it. God allows all late comers a chance to pass and treats everyone equally. But I wouldn't wait too long, because the exam will become more difficult as more clever tests and less subtle methods are employed.

The Book of Revelation and other Scripture about the Last Days give clues about the tests we will be given. Everything from an antichrist who will deceive the world into sin to unparalleled natural disasters to plagues not seen since the days of the Old Testament.

They include some very difficult ordeals, but if I have learned anything about the Last Days, the most important lesson is that the Faithful have absolutely nothing to fear. Our job is simply to stay on God's path with diligence, vigilance, discernment, and wisdom.

For you know very well that the day of the Lord will come

[unexpectedly] like a thief in the night...

But you, brothers, are not in darkness so that this day should surprise you like a thief...

For God did not appoint us to suffer wrath but to receive salvation through our Lord Jesus Christ. He died for us so that, whether we are awake or asleep, we may live together with him...

Do not put out the Spirit's fire; do not treat prophecies with contempt. Test everything. Hold on to the good. Avoid every kind of evil. 1 Thessalonians 5:2

And remember, until the circle is completed to 360 degrees and His kingdom comes literally to earth, *"The kingdom of God is within you."* Luke 17:20. That is, it is by your spiritual renewal through Grace that the kingdom of heaven is realized on earth. Walking towards your personal heaven, your overall good, in this life is only a matter of accepting God's hand offered in Grace.

References

Comfort, Ray. *Scientific Facts in the Bible*. Gainsville,
Florida: Bridge-Logos, 2001. Print.

Lucado, Max. *Just Like Jesus*. Nashville,
Tennessee: Thomas Nelson, 1998. Print.

n.p. *NASA*. National Aeronautics and Space Administration,
2009. Web. 14 April 2009.
< http://www.nasa.gov>.

Nelson, Roger. *Global Consciousness Project (EGG)*.
Princeton U, 2009. Web. 1 April 2009.
< http://noosphere.princeton.edu>.

Sauzek, Roy. *Take His Heart*. Take His Heart Ministries,
2009. Web. 3 November 2009.
< http://www.takehisheart.com>.

Strobel, Lee. *The Case for Christ*. Grand Rapids,
Michigan: Zondervan, 1998. Print.

Insert 1: "San Giorgio Maggiore at Dusk" by Claude Monet (1908), which shows the monastery island of San Giorgio as seen from the southest end of Venice.

Insert 2: Ty's 2004 airbrushed motorcycle tank mural

Insert 3: Ty and his Triumph Daytona on the race track
Photo courtesy Momentum Motorsports Photography